T.

2004

TAURUS
2004

Jane Struthers

p

This is a Parragon Book
First published in 2003

Parragon
Queen Street House
4 Queen Street
Bath BA1 1HE
UK

Produced by Magpie Books, an imprint of
Constable & Robinson Ltd, London

© Jane Struthers 2003

Illustrations courtesy of Slatter-Anderson, London
Cover courtesy of Simon Levy

ISBN 1-40541-570-3

A copy of the British Library Cataloguing-in-Publication Data
is available from the British Library

Printed and bound in the EU

CONTENTS

Dates for 2004

Taurus 21 April – 21 May

Gemini 22 May – 21 June

Cancer 22 June – 22 July

Leo 23 July – 23 August

Virgo 24 August – 23 September

Libra 24 September – 23 October

Scorpio 24 October – 22 November

Sagittarius 23 November – 21 December

Capricorn 22 December – 20 January

Aquarius 21 January – 18 February

Pisces 19 February – 20 March

Aries 21 March – 20 April

INTRODUCTION

Dear Taurus

Happy New Year! I hope that 2004 is everything you want it to be, and more. If you're a clever Taurean you'll want to make the very best of the opportunities coming your way in the year ahead, which is why this book is so useful. It will help you to maximize your many chances and show you how to deal with any problem areas that you encounter.

My summary of 2004 in **The Year 2004** tells you exactly what you can expect in your relationships, health, money and career this year, and how to make the most of them. This is followed by my day-by-day forecasts for 2004, complete with at-a-glance charts that show you the general trend for each month.

Being born under the sign of Taurus gives you a special set of characteristics, and you can read all about them in **Your Taurus Sun Sign**. It's divided into four sections describing your relationships, health, money and career, so you can get a thorough insight into your personality. If some of your relationships have been puzzling you recently, you need to read **Love and the Stars** to discover what's going on. It describes your compatibility with each of the twelve signs, and is followed by two charts that show how you get on with the other signs in love and sex, and also as friends.

Everyone needs to get away from it all every now and then, and holidays can be good for our health. If you've ever wondered about the ideal holiday for your Taurus Sun sign, turn to **Your Astrological Holiday Guide** to discover which destinations and activities will suit you best.

If you were born at the beginning or end of Taurus you may have always wondered if you're really a Taurean or whether you're an Arien or a Gemini instead. Well, you can finally solve the mystery by turning to **Born on the Cusp?** and discovering which is your true Sun sign.

This book is all you need to get the very best out of 2004, so have fun and make it a great year!

Jane Struthers

THE YEAR 2004

 Friends and Lovers

The emotional atmosphere is looking pretty rosy as 2004 gets under way. Friends and lovers can't get enough of you, you seem blessed with abundant charm and, generally speaking, things are going really well for you. If you're a solo Taurean who's starting to feel dusty from being on the shelf for a while, never mind because you could soon be in great demand. Who knows, you might even struggle to juggle all the suitors who come your way! And it won't just be romantic love that brightens up your life in 2004 – you'll also get even more pleasure than usual from being with some of your favourite people.

Close relationships have been carrying quite a punch in recent years and they haven't finished with you yet. This is especially true if you were born between 9 and 12 May, when 2004 will be a year of intense emotions and new levels of intimacy with you-know-who. You might even meet someone new and realize that your paths were destined to cross.

Friends will keep you on your toes this year, behaving in ways that keep you guessing about what their next move will be. Don't expect your chums to be predictable because that's the last thing that will happen now. There's even a chance that you could be smitten by someone who's been a chum until now, or that you'll become friends with the sort of person you'd normally cross the road to avoid. Anything goes in 2004!

Health

You're feeling great in 2004! In fact, you may not have felt this good for quite some time, so make the most of it. Between January and late September you'll be in celebratory mood and will want to cram in as much enjoyment as possible. This will do you the world of good, provided of course that you don't go over the top and end up suffering from the ill effects of too much rich food and drink. You won't have much will-power, so, given the choice between finishing off a bar of chocolate or putting it back in the drawer for another day, you'll soon be throwing the wrapper in the dustbin and telling yourself that you'll start your diet tomorrow.

Unfortunately, you'll still be at risk of putting on too much weight from late September until the end of the year. Ideally, you should get a moderate amount of exercise during this time to avoid having to buy a completely new wardrobe because you can't fit into your clothes any more.

If you decide that you need to take yourself in hand, the best time to do this is in October, when all your efforts seem to carry extra impact and any resolutions you make stand an excellent chance of lasting.

Money

Be careful if you've decided that you need to draw in your horns financially because it will be difficult to make this happen between January and late September. That's because there will be so many tempting things to spend your money on, particularly if they'll bring you a lot of enjoyment. So you might splash out a lot of cash on entertainment, leisure activities, restaurants and anything else that brings a happy smile to your lips. You'll feel very generous, too, and will want to make sure everyone else shares in the fun, which could make it even more expensive.

It's very important that you ensure your finances are in apple-pie order this year and that you keep on the right side of officialdom, so try to avoid getting in a mess with your income tax return or running up massive credit card debts. The results are likely to be difficult and uncomfortable, and it will be hard to shake them off.

If you've decided that you don't earn enough money in your current job, look for something new from late September onwards. You'll be very pleased that you did!

Career

Make the most of your many talents in 2004! The first nine months of the year are marvellous for giving full rein to your artistic and creative abilities: not only will this be satisfying but it will also help to put you in the limelight. And that's exactly where you need to be in 2004. If your job doesn't give you much opportunity to express the inner you, then do so through an enjoyable hobby. You never know – what begins as a hobby might end up as a lucrative string to your bow in the years to come.

Colleagues and customers are very helpful and congenial from late September onwards. It will be a good time to work with others, and also to do your bit to ensure that the atmosphere is as enjoyable as possible. This is also a terrific opportunity to look for a better job if that's one of the things you've promised yourself for 2004. You'll be especially lucky at this if you start looking in earnest in October.

Although your job prospects are looking great this year, you should exercise caution in believing everything you're told. During the next few years you'll have to cope with times when the people you thought you could trust turn out to be deceitful or manipulative, so it's very important for you not to let anyone pull the wool over your eyes. Be especially wary of anyone who pretends to be holier-than-thou when all the time they're really plotting and conniving to steal a march on everyone around them.

Your Day by Day Guide

JANUARY AT A GLANCE

Love	❤ ❤ ❤
Money	£ $
Career	💻 💻 💻 💻 💻
Health	☼ ☼

• *Thursday 1 January* •

You want it to be a nice, enjoyable start to 2004 but first you've got to deal with a certain person who seems determined to throw a spanner in the works. You strongly suspect that they're trying to stymie you in some way, even if you can't work out why. If you feel you're making no headway with them at all, leave them to stew in their own juice while you get on with other things.

• *Friday 2 January* •

Life is looking pretty good today and you're feeling very positive. The prospect of travel is really appealing, especially if you don't have anything planned for the next few months. So how about investigating the offers at your local travel agent's? You could score a double whammy by snapping up a bargain and having something wonderful to look forward to.

• *Saturday 3 January* •

Ahem. I hate to mention this so early in the year but how are your finances looking? If you're already flat broke, having spent too much money last month (and possibly yesterday, too), you should avoid the shops like the plague today because you'll be very tempted to splash out on all sorts of impulse buys. But if you can't see them, you can't buy them. Simple!

• *Sunday 4 January* •

Someone you respect could give you some good advice about your finances today. However, there might be a certain amount of wishful thinking or idealism wrapped up in it, so you'll have to be selective about what you choose to believe and what you choose to reject. If you haven't seen an older friend or relative lately they'll be delighted to hear from you now.

• *Monday 5 January* •

You want to help others today, especially if you believe that they can't look after themselves very well or you would like to share some of your bounty with them. You'll be especially attracted to good causes and charitable ventures, and you may even decide to pledge your support through regular donations or offers of your time.

• *Tuesday 6 January* •

People behave in ways you aren't expecting today, so be prepared for some unforeseen events. These are unlikely to cause you problems so don't worry about them. Instead, be prepared to go with the flow. This isn't always easy for typical Taureans but right now you feel you've got nothing to lose and you're intrigued to know what's going to happen next.

• *Wednesday 7 January* •

During the next two weeks it will be very important to separate the rhetoric from the facts. So try not to be swayed by arguments that have more to do with the way someone would like the world to be than with life as we know it. This will be even more timely advice if you've got to make decisions about a child's future. You can't afford to take risks or rely on wishful thinking.

• *Thursday 8 January* •

Communications could go haywire today, especially if you're making contact with someone for the first time or you've got to write an important letter. If possible, try to postpone any important correspondence or communication until tomorrow, which looks much more favourable. Right now, things could get bogged down through crossed wires or even someone's blank indifference.

• *Friday 9 January* •

You're feeling confident and self-assured, and as a result things are almost bound to go well. In fact, this looks like being one of the most positive and enjoyable days of the entire month, so make the most of it. A golden opportunity could come your way, in which case you'll really be missing out if you don't take advantage of it. It's time to rise to a challenge!

• *Saturday 10 January* •

A certain member of the family is in danger of getting lost in a world of nostalgia today, and they'll expect you to join them there. Their mood means that there'll be a nasty atmosphere if you refuse, so you'll probably have to do the tactful thing and pretend to stroll down memory lane with them before changing the subject as quickly as possible.

• *Sunday 11 January* •

You're in a very practical mood and you want to make every second count. This means you could be pretty busy getting on with the mundane chores. Today is also a very good day for chivvying along anyone who's supposed to doing something for you. Yet you'll manage to do this with tremendous diplomacy, so no one will feel that they're being nagged or hurried.

• Monday 12 January •

You take great pleasure in getting on well with everyone you meet today, and there may even be times when you'll go out of your way to keep someone sweet. Rather than feeling that this is somehow demeaning, you'll be delighted to know that you've averted a row. Besides, at the moment you're prepared to take people as you find them, warts and all. Good for you!

• Tuesday 13 January •

Yesterday you were sunny-tempered and easy-going, but it isn't quite that simple today. Instead, you're likely to get very irritated by someone who you feel is taking advantage of you in some way. Maybe they're expecting you to pay for something that they want to buy, or perhaps you feel they're unfairly relying on your good nature. You'll soon snap at them.

• Wednesday 14 January •

Friends make your world go round between now and early February. It's a wonderful excuse to get together with as many chums as possible, or to concentrate on a select few. If you've been hoping that a friendship is going to develop into something much more intimate, your hopes could be realized during the next few weeks. Yippee!

• Thursday 15 January •

There's absolutely no knowing what a certain person is up to right now, nor what they're going to do. They're being a law unto themselves, which you might find rather worrying. For a start, they're showing a very independent streak which may make you wonder where you fit into their life. Try to take it all in your stride and wait to see what happens before getting into a panic.

• *Friday 16 January* •

This is a super day for your social life because everyone you meet is being cheerful and happy-go-lucky. Do your best to get out and about as much as possible – you could make some interesting contacts along the way. A loved one might also make some helpful suggestions or offer to do you a favour, for which you'll be grateful.

• *Saturday 17 January* •

This is turning out to be a terrific start to the New Year, particularly where your social life is concerned. And this is another day when things go well and people are being chummy. You're also feeling very open-minded about everyone you encounter, so you're happy to take them as they are. You'll enjoy the differences between you rather than feeling threatened by them.

• *Sunday 18 January* •

Someone is seized by an extravagant streak today, especially if they're devising a budget. If you're expected to put your money into this scheme you'll have a few things to say about it, such as 'How can we afford it?' or 'Stop right there!' Try to do this with good humour, as that will help to keep the atmosphere sweet, and avoid being provoked into exaggerations.

• Monday 19 January •

This is a marvellous day for rolling up your sleeves and getting on with any tasks that have been hanging fire lately because you've been putting them off for some reason. Today you want to work your way through them all, and you'll enjoy the glow of satisfaction that follows. You'll have good reason to feel pleased with yourself.

• Tuesday 20 January •

If you're still feeling chuffed after everything that you accomplished yesterday, you'll want to do even more today. Right now, there's no stopping you, but try not to get carried away to such an extent that you start to make decisions for other people without consulting them first. This won't go down well and you might even trigger a massive power battle, so be careful.

• Wednesday 21 January •

Today's New Moon is asking you how you're getting on with your New Year resolutions. You're in the perfect position to implement some of them, and they'll have the power of the New Moon to give them the best possible start. The coming fortnight will also be an excellent chance to push ahead with career plans or to put yourself in the spotlight.

• Thursday 22 January •

Although you usually pride yourself on being pragmatic and unruffled, it will be horribly easy for worries to nag away at you today and for your imagination to run riot as a result. So do your very best to stick to the facts and to take as constructive an approach to them as possible. It may help to discuss your thoughts with others, but don't let them depress you even further.

• *Friday 23 January* •

A friend brings you some much-needed light relief today. They might behave in very wacky and silly ways that can't help but make you laugh, or they could plan a jaunt on the spur of the moment and persuade you to join them. Be prepared to cast caution to the winds for once and to let your hair down. Right now, you could do with it!

• *Saturday 24 January* •

This is another good day for enjoying your friendships. It's great for being with kindred spirits because they'll be such relaxing company and it will be wonderful not to have to explain yourself. Any form of group activity will go well, and there's a chance that you'll be rather attracted to one of the other participants. If so, are you going to take it any further?

• *Sunday 25 January* •

Someone dear to your heart is likely to get carried away today and come on a bit strong. For instance, they might indulge in lots of wild claims or exaggerations, which you will have to take with a pinch of salt. Be wary about believing everything you hear now because people are making promises that they simply won't be able to keep, no matter how sincere they are about them at the moment.

• *Monday 26 January* •

It's a day for confidences and secrets, and you could be on the receiving end of someone's innermost thoughts. Before they start to unburden themselves to you, check that you're happy to listen to them and that you'll be able to keep their story to yourself. The same rules apply if you're confiding in someone else – make sure you can trust them before you start talking.

• *Tuesday 27 January* •

Someone has a habit of speaking out of turn or dropping clangers today, and it will start to get on your nerves after a while. Are they being deliberately blunt or offensive, or can't they help it? Do your best to hold on to your sense of humour unless you hear things that you really aren't prepared to tolerate.

• *Wednesday 28 January* •

No matter what else you do today, try to find the time for one of your favourite hobbies. It will be a great way to unwind. You might even be interested in a pastime that you've never tried before but which suddenly appeals to you. Speaking of things happening suddenly, a chum could issue a last-minute invitation that's far too tempting to turn down.

• *Thursday 29 January* •

Get into a social setting and you'll be the life and soul of the party. You'll find it just as easy to chat to strangers as to talk to people you know well. This is also a fabulous day for your love life, with a special person making a massive fuss of you. Valentine's Day might be a huge anti-climax after what happens now! Cupid is definitely on your side!

• *Friday 30 January* •

Take your mind on a journey of exploration. You're in the mood to be intrigued, thrilled and fascinated, whether that happens from reading a book, chatting to someone or watching an edge-of-the-seat programme on TV. It's also a good day for making contact with people who live far away, so ring them up or send them an e-mail, just to let them know that you're alive and kicking.

• *Saturday 31 January* •

As far as you're concerned today, someone's brain is by far the sexiest part of them. You may not always feel this way but right now you're very attracted to people who are intelligent, witty and good conversationalists. You might even be smitten by someone you meet now, who weaves a magic spell over you with words alone.

FEBRUARY AT A GLANCE

Love	♥ ♥ ♥
Money	£ $
Career	💻 💻 💻 💻 💻
Health	☼ ☼

• *Sunday 1 February* •

Watch out today because someone could exert a lot of emotional pressure on you, and it seems that they don't care how hard they put the squeeze on provided it gets results. But will it? You're unlikely to want to cave in to their demands, especially if you suspect that such a tactic will send them the message that you can be easily bullied. Yet standing up to them won't be easy, and could require some guts. Not an easy day.

• *Monday 2 February* •

This is a difficult day if you've got to concentrate on anything official, fiddly, or which will affect your reputation, because you'll really struggle with it. You could be distracted by other things or you may simply find plenty of excuses for postponing it. However, you'll excel at any activities that involve using your imagination or your humanitarian instincts.

• *Tuesday 3 February* •

You're filled with dynamic energy and vitality from today, and this happy state of affairs will last until the middle of next month. This is exactly the boost you need if you want to make lots of progress in some part of your life or you've got to muster plenty of enthusiasm and initiative. But don't overlook the need for a little finesse every now and then. You can't just barge your way into things without considering the feelings of others.

• *Wednesday 4 February* •

Today you encounter someone who's opinionated and has a lot to say for themselves. As a result, you could be treated to a lecture that you didn't want, or be regaled with all sorts of useless facts and figures. Be wary of letting your conversation stray into politics, religion or anything else that might cause offence or lead to an argument.

• *Thursday 5 February* •

A certain person may be dear to your heart but they're being very bombastic today, which you won't like at all. They could also be feeling angry about something and will goad you until you lose your temper with them. Be very careful if you suspect that you're behaving in this way yourself because it could lead to bad feelings. If you're annoyed about something then say so!

• *Friday 6 February* •

Today's Full Moon is urging you to sort out problems on the home front before they become any more fraught or tricky. The coming fortnight is also a good opportunity to accept that certain areas of your life belong to the past and that you have to move on from them. This decision will undoubtedly arouse some poignant emotions but you'll also realize that it makes a lot of sense.

• *Saturday 7 February* •

During the next two weeks you need to think carefully about your goals and the general direction that your life is taking. If you think you've got sidetracked or you're heading into a cul-de-sac, start considering how you can get yourself back into a more favourable position. It may help to pick the brains of someone you respect or who has the experience you need.

• *Sunday 8 February* •

You enter a deeply romantic and highly sensitive phase from today, and this will last until the beginning of March. Just what you need with Valentine's Day only round the corner! There's a chance that you could be drawn into a hush-hush relationship, perhaps because one or both of you is already committed elsewhere. If so, you'll find the whole situation quite glamorous.

• *Monday 9 February* •

Someone is being very outspoken, particularly if they're in a position of power or influence over you, or think they are. They might boss you about or give you the sharp edge of their tongue. Think twice before behaving in the same way – it will create a lot of animosity and you may have to end up apologizing for your bombastic attitude.

• *Tuesday 10 February* •

Do your best to stay positive today. Otherwise you'll end up feeling that you've got the cares of the world on your shoulders. Responsibilities could be weighing heavily on you, and you may tell yourself that it's your moral duty to accept them all. To make matters worse, you're probably feeling tired and worried. Do you really have to make yourself a workhorse like this? Or are you making mountains out of molehills?

• Wednesday 11 February •

You're capable of achieving a tremendous amount today, thanks to your single-mindedness and determination to make things happen. If necessary you'll be quite clinical and detached, because you'll know that that's the only way to make progress or retain your objectivity. It's an especially good day to sort out tax problems or other red tape.

• Thursday 12 February •

Even though you often pride yourself on taking things gently, that isn't the way you're behaving today. Rather, you've got a tendency to rush into things without thinking them through first and then get irritable if they don't work out in the way you wanted. You'll make much more progress if you can slow down and not charge at everything like a bull at a gate.

• Friday 13 February •

There's a rather testy atmosphere today, with certain people apparently eager to have a row or get into a strop. Unfortunately, it seems that you'll be all too happy to join them and the results will be a free-for-all, with everyone shouting their heads off. This may be the only solution if you need to clear the air, but even so you should avoid letting things get out of hand or saying anything that you'll regret when you calm down again.

• *Saturday 14 February* •

The emotional atmosphere is rather chilly today, much to your disappointment. Maybe your beloved is too busy to see you, or a social event is delayed or postponed, making you feel wretched and sorry for yourself. Do your best to avoid imagining that things are worse than they really are because, once that happens, you'll start to feel dreadfully depressed.

• *Sunday 15 February* •

Be careful if you've got to deal with anything complicated or official because, unless you can make a supreme effort, your mind won't be on the job. Instead, it will be wandering in about fifteen different directions at once and you'll really struggle to concentrate. You may also misread important information or miss some glaring errors, so doublecheck everything you do.

• *Monday 16 February* •

After a tense few days, thank goodness you're now feeling much more cheerful. Do something energetic to blow away the cobwebs and make you feel in control of your life once more. You're in an adventurous mood and will enjoy doing something that presents you with a bit of a challenge. You could also be fired up about an environmental or political cause.

• *Tuesday 17 February* •

Once again you're in ebullient good spirits and want to get as much out of the day as possible. Although you'll be happiest if you can have a change of scene, you'll also be pleased with yourself if you can use your cheerful mood to get through any tasks that are overdue and which you've therefore been avoiding. You'll be so pleased with yourself!

• Wednesday 18 February •

You need to pussyfoot around a certain person today because they've got steam coming out of their ears and they're likely to blow a gasket at the slightest provocation. Maybe they've been pushed to the limit of their endurance, so bear that in mind if their ire is directed at you. Have you been irritating them, perhaps without realizing it?

• Thursday 19 February •

During the coming four weeks you'll enjoy concentrating on your plans for the future, especially if you can start turning some of them into reality. This will also be a marvellous opportunity to get the maximum amount of enjoyment out of your friendships, so try to throw yourself into the social swing whenever possible. You might even make some new chums now.

• Friday 20 February •

You're showing a strong streak of empathy and understanding towards others today. You could decide to donate some of your time or money to a charity or voluntary project, or you might help someone you know who is finding life difficult at the moment. If you're at work you'll excel at any tasks that use your imagination or artistic skills.

• Saturday 21 February •

If you've been worried about your relationship with a friend, perhaps because things aren't going very well between you or there's been a disagreement, today is a really good day to do something about it. You'll find it easy to say what you think without going over the top and being brusque or rude. You'll also be amenable to the idea of negotiation and compromise.

• *Sunday 22 February* •

Forget all about being a tradition-loving Taurean – today you're eager to cast convention aside and show another aspect to your character. This could come as a surprise to some people, but try to take their amazed reactions in your stride. It might even come as a surprise to you, as you find yourself acting and talking in ways that would normally never occur to you.

• *Monday 23 February* •

You're in rather a sentimental mood and may also be feeling emotionally fragile. As a result, you could over-react if you think someone is being hurtful or not taking your emotions into account. Do your best not to turn tiny hiccups into massive dramas, and try to keep your feelings in perspective. If you don't, you'll end the day exhausted and overwrought.

• *Tuesday 24 February* •

Try to be as honest as possible with yourself about your motives today, particularly if things seem to be unravelling around you. Are you subconsciously sabotaging yourself in some way, perhaps by choosing projects that are doomed to failure from the outset? If so, what are you going to do about it? Think carefully before deciding.

• *Wednesday 25 February* •

Between now and mid-March your favourite choice of companions will be people who are witty and intelligent. Someone could have film star good looks but these will be wasted on you if they can't string a sentence together. If your social life is looking a bit lacklustre, consider joining a club or society that caters for one of your hobbies.

● *Thursday 26 February* ●

You're being very bouncy and playful, and you've also got a lot more energy than usual. You certainly won't want to laze around if you can possibly avoid it so try to keep as active as possible. Sporty or athletic activities are very appealing now and give you a chance to indulge in some healthy competition. Enjoy yourself but don't pull a muscle!

● *Friday 27 February* ●

Your feelings run very deep today, leading to heightened emotions and some intense moments. This is a marvellous chance to get together with your one true love because it will be a memorable occasion, and your relationship might even reach a new level of intimacy or trust. There could also be important changes to your financial situation, although you may want to keep these under your hat for the time being.

● *Saturday 28 February* ●

Business and pleasure don't mix today, and neither do love and money. In fact, they'll lead to a nasty atmosphere or the feeling that somehow you've been taken for a ride. If you're going out on the tiles with friends, make sure that you've all got a rough idea of how much it's going to cost ahead of time to avoid pleas of poverty when the bill arrives.

● *Sunday 29 February* ●

Your brain is working like clockwork right now, and it feels great. You're thinking along very practical and rational lines, which is just what you need if you want to reach an important decision or weigh up the pros and cons of a forthcoming project. You'll also shine if you're taking part in a debate or you want to put forward your point of view. No one will be able to match you for articulate delivery and clarity of vision.

MARCH AT A GLANCE

Love	❤ ❤ ❤ ❤
Money	£ $ £
Career	💻 💻
Health	☼ ☼ ☼

• *Monday 1 March* •

It's one of those days when your social life is a real joy. Everyone is being very friendly towards you, and you're being equally chummy in return. There's tremendous understanding between you, making you receptive to each other's ideas and happy to create a harmonious atmosphere. If a group gathering gets off the ground today it stands every chance of being a roaring success.

• *Tuesday 2 March* •

Life is keeping you busy and you'll enjoy dashing around from one thing to another. You're blessed with plenty of energy right now and you're making the most of it. Today is a good opportunity to keep active, so consider walking to your destination instead of getting in the car, or getting some exercise on your bicycle.

• *Wednesday 3 March* •

Is someone being a little too sensitive for their own good? It seems that way, because you're trying to choose your words carefully and not upset a certain person. Even if you secretly think they're making a meal of it or only trying to draw attention to themselves, you must still consider their feelings and avoid hurting them.

• *Thursday 4 March* •

It's a really exciting day because you're seized with enthusiasm and imagination, and your thoughts are running wild. Problems or obstacles that seemed to restrict you in the past have suddenly vanished, and you feel you've got a free rein to do almost anything you want. This is an intoxicating prospect, so what are you going to do first?

• *Friday 5 March* •

As a Taurean you're already one of the most attractive members of the zodiac, and from today you get the chance to gild the lily. Maybe you fancy changing your hairstyle, buying some new make-up, or treating yourself to some new clothes? The compliments you'll receive will probably spur you on to even greater improvements and embellishments during the month ahead.

• *Saturday 6 March* •

Today's Full Moon is sounding a sober note because it will affect some of your close relationships during the next two weeks. You might have to have a quiet word with a certain person because you aren't happy with the way they're behaving or you think your relationship could do with some first aid. When dealing with children, you may have to be stricter than usual.

• *Sunday 7 March* •

You're feeling playful, dynamic and happy-go-lucky today, and long may it last! You won't want to sit around staring at the wall if you can possibly avoid it, and you'll jump at the chance of having an adventure or doing something exciting. One of your favourite people will be great company and there could also be a sexy interlude at some point. It's going to be quite a day!

• *Monday 8 March* •

A friend wants to get in touch with you because they've got a suggestion for you. It will be definitely worth your while to listen to them, even if you eventually decide not to take up their offer. However, there's every indication that you'll leap at what they're proposing and will want to set it in motion as soon as possible.

• *Tuesday 9 March* •

Yet again, friends brighten up your day, especially if you're with people who are slightly out of the ordinary or who always spur you into action. Don't be surprised if a chum gets in touch out of the blue or invites you to do something that would never otherwise have occurred to you. If you're going to a group event you could be attracted to someone you meet there.

• *Wednesday 10 March* •

The atmosphere between you and a certain someone is highly charged today, which may or may not be a good thing. It could be great if it throws you into each other's arms after a period of stress or misunderstanding, but it may not be such good news if it provokes a lot of tension. So do your best to control your emotions and not let them control you.

• *Thursday 11 March* •

This is a wonderful day to concentrate on putting plans into action, particularly if they concern neighbourhood affairs or close members of the family. Things are going very smoothly and important people are being co-operative, making you optimistic about the future. You might also have a very constructive conversation with someone you'll come to rely on.

• *Friday 12 March* •

During the rest of the month you'll relish the prospect of having some time to yourself, so you can think things through. Your thoughts will run along very contemplative lines and you may even get involved with an activity that emphasizes this, such as meditation. You'll also guard your privacy carefully and will be careful about what you say, and to whom you say it.

• *Saturday 13 March* •

Any hint of possessiveness on your part will go down like the proverbial lead balloon today, leading to some tempestuous scenes. Yet you'll feel driven to do or say something if you are feeling threatened or disturbed by a partner's behaviour, no matter what the consequences. Indeed, you may have decided that anything is better than inaction or allowing the situation to continue.

• *Sunday 14 March* •

You're in an extremely rational and logical mood today, with your brain working even better than usual. If you want to make a decision now you'll be able to do so with accuracy and detachment. The question is whether you'll be too remote and precise, making certain people feel that you're being cold-blooded or are lacking in compassion. Do they have a point?

• *Monday 15 March* •

This is another day when your brain is working well and you're able to examine difficult situations from several angles. However, you'll have to be very firm with yourself if you want to avoid letting hidden fears and worries move to the front of your mind and then dominate your thoughts. If this does happen, look your worries in the face and work out exactly what you should do about them.

• *Tuesday 16 March* •

You're in a terrific mood today and are feeling outgoing and sociable. Ideally, you should get together with people who will make you laugh, and who share your current optimism and foresight. If you meet someone you don't know very well, make an effort to draw them out and get them talking. They could turn out to be a fascinating companion.

• *Wednesday 17 March* •

This promises to be a highly enjoyable day, especially if you've got something to celebrate. You're in high spirits and so you'll get as much fun out of every situation you encounter as possible. Laughter won't be very far away, either. As for your love life . . . Let's just say that one of your dreams could come true now, and that you'll be dancing on air as a result.

• *Thursday 18 March* •

You're ready to throw yourself into your social life and you'll feel cheated if you can't spend time with friends or other kindred spirits. This is the perfect day to organize a forthcoming social event as you've currently got the energy to make things happen or chase people up if you're waiting to hear from them, and you'll come up with exciting new plans, too.

• *Friday 19 March* •

Be careful because misunderstandings are rife today, especially when you're dealing with people who have power or authority over you. Maybe they're sending out a confusing message or you feel you can't trust them. You might even suspect that they're trying to trip you up in some way. So tread carefully and try to steer clear of potential troublemakers.

• *Saturday 20 March* •

Over the coming fortnight you'll value any chance of privacy and solitude. It's not that you'll be feeling dramatically anti-social, more that you'll shine better in social situations if you can alternate them with periods of peace and quiet. This is a marvellous chance to catch your breath and recharge your batteries, so try to get as much rest and relaxation as possible.

• *Sunday 21 March* •

Between now and early May you'll want to spend a lot of time and effort on improving your finances. You could look for ways to boost your investments or you might instigate quite an aggressive economy drive. Unfortunately, if your ideas don't match those of the people around you, there could be a lot of tension but you'll be determined to stand your ground and not back down.

• *Monday 22 March* •

You're touched by someone's plight today and want to help them in some way. This might happen when you read a charity appeal and decide to donate some money, or you could realize that someone in your immediate social circle is badly in need of help and that charity begins closer to home. You'll lend a hand but won't want to make a big song and dance about it. Good for you!

• *Tuesday 23 March* •

If you're currently on a fact-finding mission then you'll make a lot of progress today. Your mind is as sharp as a razor and you won't want to waste time on any extraneous information or frivolous diversions. This is also a good day for taking part in a discussion or tactful conversation: you'll be able to get your point across without hurting anyone else's feelings.

• *Wednesday 24 March* •

Your curiosity will be aroused at the merest hint of a mystery today, and after that you'll be like a bloodhound on the trail of an elusive scent. So if someone is being enigmatic, or you can't help wondering what they're up to, you'll start to behave like Sherlock Holmes at his best. But make sure you know when to mind your own business; otherwise you might stray into murky waters and find that you're out of your depth.

• *Thursday 25 March* •

The most important thing on your mind right now is money, and it's influencing your moods more than you realize. So you might soon lose your temper if you're currently feeling broke, or you could get irritated if you suspect that someone is trying to pull a fast one. If you're out shopping you'll be remorseless in your drive to strike a bargain or get a good deal.

• *Friday 26 March* •

A small but persistent voice is nagging away at you and it will be almost impossible to escape. What is it? It's the voice of your conscience, and it's an uncomfortable companion right now. Use it as a spur to make amends if needs be, or to get overdue projects out of the way, but try not to let it make you feel ineffectual, impotent or full of self-loathing. Keep a sense of perspective!

• *Saturday 27 March* •

Spare a few minutes today to keep track of your finances, such as checking your bank statement or filling in the stubs in your chequebook. This won't take very long and it will be good to get it out of the way. If you're shopping, you'll prefer to be left to your own devices at some point, especially if you want to buy something away from the prying eyes of others.

• *Sunday 28 March* •

People are being very moody and crotchety today, so take care. You might inadvertently say the wrong thing and then wonder why you're on the receiving end of so much flak. If you're brooding about something, either take some constructive action over it or let it go. Above all, avoid taking it out on people who have no connection with it, because that wouldn't be fair.

• *Monday 29 March* •

An invitation might come your way now, in which case it will make your day and give you something nice to look forward to. Alternatively, how about issuing a few invitations of your own, even if you're only inviting some friends out for a drink?

You're in an extravagant mood right now and won't want to stint yourself, so bear that in mind if you're spending money.

• *Tuesday 30 March* •

You're blessed with oodles of charm today, so make the most of your current diplomacy. If a neighbour or close relative hasn't been the easiest company recently, this is a good opportunity to sweeten them up and find out what's wrong. If you're the cause of their grumpiness then make sure you apologize, as this could work wonders. But be sincere about it!

• *Wednesday 31 March* •

You value your home comforts even more than usual today, and you're also feeling quite sentimental and emotional. In an ideal world, you would stay in familiar surroundings now, preferably in the company of loved ones. If that isn't possible, make contact with some of your nearest and dearest and arrange to see them as soon as you can.

APRIL AT A GLANCE

Love	♥ ♥ ♥ ♥ ♥
Money	£ $ £ $
Career	💻 💻 💻 💻 💻
Health	☼ ☼ ☼ ☼ ☼

• *Thursday 1 April* •

During the next few days your thoughts will revolve around yourself and your own concerns, making it quite difficult at times to concentrate on anyone else's problems. That's just the way it is at the moment, although you may have to disguise the worst excesses of your temporary self-absorption to avoid hurting anyone or giving them the impression that you don't care about them. Of course you do, but you've got other things to think about right now.

• *Friday 2 April* •

It's going to be a super day, because everyone is being friendly and affectionate. Don't expect anything major to happen, but you'll certainly enjoy yourself by doing ordinary things with some of your favourite people. If you feel like going out on the town you'll get a kick out of going dancing, bowling or visiting the cinema.

• *Saturday 3 April* •

An extravagant phase starts to sneak up on you today and it won't let you go for several weeks yet. This means you'll have to count the pennies carefully if you're currently trying to be sensible with your cash, otherwise you'll be splashing it around as though it's going out of style. If you can afford it, you'll enjoy buying items that are luxurious, sophisticated or glamorous.

• *Sunday 4 April* •

If you need help or advice, someone will be there to lend a hand now. They might be someone tangible, such as a older relative or friend, who can give you some guidance. On the other hand, you might get the powerful feeling that you're being given help by forces beyond your comprehension, such as a guardian angel.

• *Monday 5 April* •

During the next two weeks you'll have to think very carefully about your health and general well-being. If you're currently feeling under par or there is more of you than you'd like, it's time to do something about it. Maybe you need to seek medical advice or take yourself in hand in some way. Questions about your working life may also need to be resolved now.

• *Tuesday 6 April* •

Communications won't always be easy for the rest of April, and there will be occasions when wires get crossed and everyone gets in a muddle. Do your best not to make things worse than they need be, by being as straightforward and honest as possible. Avoid the temptation to hedge your bets or sit on the fence; if you do, people will impose their own interpretations on your motives.

• *Wednesday 7 April* •

You'll excel at any sort of team work now because you'll enjoy working with others and feeling that you're all on the same side. What's more, you'll try to make the experience as enjoyable as possible, whether that means simply being friendly, cracking some jokes, or producing a packet of chocolate biscuits at teatime.

• *Thursday 8 April* •

Financial tension is in the air, leading to some tricky moments. You might get in a bit of a stew when you realize that someone has been spending more than their fair share of the joint account, or a debt that you're owed still shows no signs of being repaid. Do your best not to let things get out of proportion, or make a scene over something that doesn't really merit it.

• *Friday 9 April* •

Watch out if you're the sort of Taurean who likes to know exactly what's happening and who panics at the prospect of the unexpected. If this sounds like you then you'll find it difficult to cope with the vagaries and strange behaviour of a certain person now. Unfortunately, they are probably deliberately winding you up, so the more you react the happier they'll be.

• *Saturday 10 April* •

You're very interested in what's going on around you today, so you'll want to keep abreast of all the latest news. Today's an especially good opportunity to catch up on the gossip with friends who live far away, so give them a ring, write them a letter or send them an e-mail. If you're currently organizing some travel plans, check that they're running smoothly.

• *Sunday 11 April* •

How honest are you with yourself? The more you're able to face up to yourself and recognize your own motives, the more productive today will be. This is a marvellous chance to subject yourself to some careful self-analysis, especially if you want to understand why certain things are happening to you at the moment. You'll gain some valuable insight into yourself as a result.

• *Monday 12 April* •

Someone's being ultra-sensitive and huffy today, so you'll feel as though you've got to tiptoe around them to avoid saying or doing the wrong thing. There may be good reason for their current mood, in which case you'll do your best to be considerate. But you won't have much patience if you suspect that they're trying it on or are attempting to manipulate you in some way.

• *Tuesday 13 April* •

Be very careful when talking about anything that's supposed to be a secret or confidential between now and the end of the month, as someone could easily let the cat out of the bag. This might be accidental or it could be malicious, but the resulting rumpus will make you wish you'd never breathed a word. So maintain a discreet silence when necessary, or face the music.

• *Wednesday 14 April* •

Money is flowing through your hands like water today, and you're loving every minute of it! Temptations abound and you simply can't resist them, whether that means treating yourself to a bar of chocolate in your lunch hour or splurging wildly on some new clothes. You'll have a ball if you can afford it, but remorse will soon follow if you can't.

• *Thursday 15 April* •

You're talking a lot of sense right now, especially when discussing subjects that are close to home or which concern everyday details. You've got your head screwed on the right way at the moment, so make the most of it by getting on with any activities that demand clear thinking and a cool head. It's an especially good day for filling in forms.

• *Friday 16 April* •

Someone could easily get hot under the collar about money matters today, and if you're wise you'll avoid provoking them for no good reason. They're already feeling short-tempered and they'll certainly lose their rag if they think you've been careless with the cash. There could also be dissent with a friend over how much something costs.

• Saturday 17 April •

A certain someone is longing to confide in you, and they'll grab any chance they can get. So they might ring up and immediately launch into a long sob story, or they could buttonhole you in person. Either way, it's highly likely that they won't know when to stop talking, and you'll end up feeling like a sitting duck. Yet you'll be too kind-hearted to shut them up.

• Sunday 18 April •

A few treats are in order today! They'll make you feel pampered and cared for, even if you have to buy them yourself. And you'll feel deliciously naughty if you know that you should really be saving your money for more prosaic items, such as the electricity bill. The best way to handle this is to buy yourself an inexpensive luxury, such as a glossy magazine, and leave it at that.

• Monday 19 April •

This is an important day for you because you'll be able to reach a decision about something that's been worrying you lately, and you're also beginning to feel much more positive and energetic than you have for some time. This will be an invigorating combination of experiences, and it's highly likely that they're connected in some way. So face up to the bugbear and you'll soon feel better.

• Tuesday 20 April •

If you want to get the most out of the day, surround yourself with some of your favourite people. You won't have to spend ages with them, either, to get the benefit of their company. If a party or some other sort of celebration is in the offing, this is a good chance to check what you'll be wearing. But you might decide that it's out of date and you need to buy something new. Oh dear!

• *Wednesday 21 April* •

Play your cards right today and you'll be amazed by the kindness and empathy of a certain person. Maybe you've always thought they were a bit stand-offish or too important to bother with you, but today's events prove that you're wrong. There could also be a strong bond between you and someone who comes from a different generation, with neither of you aware of any age gap. Great!

• *Thursday 22 April* •

You're feeling restless and want to spend your way out of trouble. However, that could lead to several problems. For a start, you might deliberately splash out on things you can't afford, and then you may not like them once you get them home. You could also be drawn to items that you hope will send shock waves through a certain person or make a big statement, and this could lead to some difficult scenes.

• *Friday 23 April* •

This is a day for counting your blessings. Once you start, you'll realize that you have many more reasons to be thankful than you might at first have imagined. You could even be inspired to spread your good fortune in the direction of people who aren't as lucky as you, perhaps by donating some money to a good cause or taking some old belongings you no longer want to a charity shop.

• *Saturday 24 April* •

Go very, very carefully when handling any sort of financial transaction or discussion because you're likely to encounter a tremendous amount of opposition and obstinacy. What's more, someone may turn the entire encounter into a battle of wills, perhaps determined to prove their independence or show that they don't have to do what you say.

• *Sunday 25 April* •

Keep your options open when you're with friends because you won't know what they're going to suggest. For instance, a chum might bring you a terrific opportunity, but you'll only realize how great it is after you've taken up their offer. If you meet someone new today they'll be unconventional in some way, which will be exactly why you were attracted to them in the first place.

• *Monday 26 April* •

Mind your Ps and Qs if you want a nice, quiet day; otherwise you'll end up treading on people's toes or causing offence. You may not even realize that you're doing it at the time because you're completely unaware of what you're saying. Or is someone being far too sensitive for their own good? It may be six of one and half a dozen of the other.

• *Tuesday 27 April* •

It seems that a certain member of the family is on the warpath. Something has got under their skin and it's rankling, and they won't be happy until they've done some shouting and stamping of feet. Unfortunately, it looks as though you're the one who's shooting from the hip. If so, make sure you get angry with the person who deserves it and not any innocent by-standers.

• *Wednesday 28 April* •

You'll enjoy putting your brain to good use today by marshalling the facts and making some informed decisions. You won't want to be rushed into anything, though, because you realize the importance of taking your time right now. You may also have to do some levelling with a neighbour or close relative, in which you gently set them straight about something.

• *Thursday 29 April* •

A loved one tries your patience to the limit today. They could pull the rug out from under you in some way or do things that are deliberately intended to rattle you. Will you crack under the strain or pretend that nothing's wrong? If you do manage to remain cool, calm and collected, make sure that you release any pent-up nervous energy at some point, or you'll start to feel very edgy and restless.

• *Friday 30 April* •

After almost a month of confusion and misunderstandings, life begins to return to a semblance of normality today. It may take a couple of days for everything to sort itself out, so consider whether you should say or do something that will improve the situation. If you're going to a social event, it will be one of the high points of the entire month.

MAY AT A GLANCE

Love	♥ ♥ ♥ ♥ ♥
Money	£ $ £ $ £
Career	💻 💻 💻 💻 💻
Health	☼ ☼ ☼ ☼ ☼

• *Saturday 1 May* •

The best way to deal with loved ones today is to be reasonable but not a pushover, and sensible without losing your sense of humour. In other words, you need to be moderate and sensitive. Mind you, your current optimism and good nature will win a lot of people over to your side and make them glad to give you their backing.

• *Sunday 2 May* •

Financial transactions flow about as easily as a lump of cement today, so take care. You might have to deal with a skilled tactician who enjoys manipulating others into doing what they want. For instance, you might encounter someone who wants something that you're selling but who will do their best not to pay for it. If you know someone who fits this description, avoid them like the plague at the moment in case they get up to their old tricks again.

• *Monday 3 May* •

Take care today because it will be horribly easy to get bogged down in details and to lose track of what's going on around you. If you're doing something complicated or fiddly, you could end up being unable to see the wood for the trees or going round in circles. The same is true if you're trying to beat the clock at work – you might slow yourself down because you're in such a hurry that you start to make silly mistakes.

• Tuesday 4 May •

Today's eclipsed Full Moon will have a powerful effect on your relationships during the next couple of weeks. If things have been going wrong between you and a certain person, matters will reach crisis point, forcing you to do something about them. Alternatively, a partnership could be transformed now, moving from one level to something totally different and even better.

• Wednesday 5 May •

Your self-confidence appears to have drained away, leaving you feeling vulnerable and unsure of yourself. You could have doubts about some of your abilities or you might wonder if you're on the right track in your career. It won't help if a certain person is whispering weasel words in your ear that are calculated to make you feel demoralized or inadequate. Don't listen to them!

• Thursday 6 May •

Watch out if you're going anywhere near the shops because you'll soon be throwing money around in all directions. You'll want to buy this, that and the other, whether or not you can afford it. You'll tell yourself that as you're using your credit or debit card anyway, you might as well buy something else with it too . . . A definite danger signal of imminent over-spending!

• Friday 7 May •

You'll be quite forthright, and at times even outspoken, between now and late June. This will be very helpful whenever you need to stand up for yourself or develop the hide of an elephant, but it could also cause problems if you're too blunt or unfeeling. So do your best to know when you should be vociferous and when it would be better to speak softly and gently.

• *Saturday 8 May* •

You don't have as much energy as usual today so keep some in reserve, just in case you need it. Maybe you're simply having an off day and can't think of anything you'd rather do than flop on the sofa or stay in bed. Or maybe there's a good reason why you're feeling drained, perhaps because you aren't very well or because you're worrying about something and it's preying on your mind.

• *Sunday 9 May* •

Do your best to have a change of scene at some point today, as this will soon make you feel rejuvenated and raring to go. Ideally, it should be somewhere that you've never visited before, and you'll enjoy it even more if it's steeped in history, art or culture. You'll also enjoy planning a forthcoming trip or holiday, and perhaps reading up about your destination.

• *Monday 10 May* •

This is a super day for thinking about who and what means the most to you in life. You might want to make a list of them so you can concentrate on them more, especially if some of them usually have to go by the wayside because of more pressing concerns. At some point you might also have a confidential chat about the state of your finances or your heart.

• *Tuesday 11 May* •

Be careful when dealing with people who are older or more influential than you – there could be a lot of tension between you. Maybe they're throwing their weight about and you don't like it, or perhaps they think you're getting above yourself and you should be more respectful towards them. Whatever is wrong, don't let it get worse than necessary.

• *Wednesday 12 May* •

Don't get your hopes up too high today or you might be disappointed about something. For instance, a loved one could make you a promise that they mean at the time but which they either forget about or can't deliver. Or they could tell you that they've seen in a particular shop the very item you've been looking for, but when you get there you realize they've made a mistake.

• *Thursday 13 May* •

It would be a shame to spend the day by yourself because you're feeling so sociable and easy-going. If possible, get together with friends at some point because you'll enjoy their company. They might also have some interesting information for you, or they could suggest an idea that really appeals to you.

• *Friday 14 May* •

If you're trying to economize at the moment, be warned: today is one of those days when money seems to leach out of your wallet without you even being aware of it. If you're meeting a friend or going out on the town, it might work out more expensive than you'd realized and you could end the evening wondering where all the money went.

• *Saturday 15 May* •

Try to keep your spirits up or you'll soon start to feel rather anxious and miserable. Maybe you hear some worrying news and can't stop thinking about it, or perhaps you're already fretting about something and get further reminders of it now. Your mood will sink very low indeed unless you can be firm with yourself and force yourself to concentrate on other things.

• *Sunday 16 May* •

Early last month you started to concentrate on personal projects for a brief spell before things went a little haywire. Well, the good news is that you get another bite at the cherry from today, and you'll be in this fortunate position until early June. So carry on from when you were so rudely interrupted by matters beyond your control. And good luck!

• *Monday 17 May* •

Financial and emotional matters will call for a careful re-evaluation between now and the end of June. You may have to reassess how much someone or something means to you, especially if you suspect that you're in danger of losing them or it. You'll also have to reconsider your values in life, asking yourself whether they are still relevant for you or if they need to be revised.

• *Tuesday 18 May* •

It's very difficult to work out what's going on today, and even harder to deal with certain people. They're being sly, elusive and distinctly shifty. They may also be confused about what they're telling you, which will be dodgy if they're supposed to be giving you orders or instructions. Doublecheck anything that sounds peculiar, just in case they've made a mistake.

• *Wednesday 19 May* •

Today sees a New Moon that will have a very exciting effect on your life during the coming fortnight. This is your chance to get new projects under way and to take the initiative on all the ideas that have come to you recently. You might also want to alter your image in some way or branch out in new directions now.

• *Thursday 20 May* •

Your values come under the spotlight from today, and events may conspire to make you think about them in a lot of detail. For instance, you might wonder whether something is worth the effort any longer, or you could realize that an essential ingredient is missing from your life. Values are very important to you, Taurus, and this is no time to treat them lightly.

• *Friday 21 May* •

People are full of surprises right now, so be prepared for any eventuality. Someone might behave in ways you weren't expecting or they could make suggestions that really set you thinking. But don't worry, because they're unlikely to shock or alarm you. Instead, you'll be amused and interested in what's going on around you.

• *Saturday 22 May* •

You're blessed with an abundance of energy and vitality today, making you eager to get out and about and to keep as busy as possible. Ideally, you should do something that burns up lots of calories and nervous energy, such as visiting the gym, going for a brisk walk, or anything else that takes your fancy. Your love life is also looking pretty vibrant right now.

• *Sunday 23 May* •

Communications go slightly skew-whiff today, and there doesn't seem to be much you can do about it except be prepared. If you've arranged to meet someone they might be late and there's even a possibility that they won't turn up at all. Your phone might go wrong, your computer could keep crashing or someone could get completely the wrong end of the stick. Aaaagh!

• *Monday 24 May* •

You'll take great pleasure from putting your brain to good use today, especially if you're rising to some sort of challenge in the process. Maybe you'll tackle a crossword puzzle, enter a brain-stretching competition or teach yourself something new. Something else that is your idea of heaven right now is to have a good gossip with one of your favourite companions, especially if you indulge in some delightful speculation about someone's motives.

• *Tuesday 25 May* •

You're capable of making slow and measured progress today. You'll find this particularly easy when taking part in discussions or negotiations. However, if you were hoping to zip your way through the chores or do everything at double speed you're going to be mightily disappointed because that isn't how things will work out at all. You'll just have to be patient.

• *Wednesday 26 May* •

This is a good day to go shopping for domestic items, such as food or home furnishings. Whether your home is big or small, grand or modest, you'll enjoy buying things that will add to its comfort and appearance. If you're keen on gardening you'll be tempted to buy some plants or possibly even some garden furniture.

• *Thursday 27 May* •

Taureans are often accused of being slightly boring and conservative, and today you're determined to break out of this limiting mould. You want to show the world a different side to your character, especially if it's one that they never imagined they'd see. So you could buy yourself something that's completely out of character but which makes you feel fantastic.

• *Friday 28 May* •

There are strange goings-on today, because there's a discrepancy between what people are saying to you and what you're hearing. For instance, someone may give you some advice and you might interpret it as criticism. Or they could tell you to do one thing but you'll do something completely different because that's what you thought they said. What's wrong?

• *Saturday 29 May* •

This is a great day for restoring your energy by doing things that make you feel and look good. You might decide to treat yourself to a massage or beauty treatment, or maybe a complementary therapy would be more in your line. If you're interested in improving your well-being, a stroll around your local health shop could be time – and money – well spent.

• *Sunday 30 May* •

Once again you'll enjoy taking care of yourself and setting yourself up for the week ahead. If your idea of heaven is to flop on the sofa all day long, then do your best to make it happen now. If you're with a colleague, you'll try to create an easy-going and relaxed atmosphere, and you may also offer to do them a favour.

• Monday 31 May •

Watch out today if you're supposed to be saving money because you're far more likely to spend it instead. Yes, it's one of those days when you've only got to see something in a shop for you to want to buy it. Although you'll enjoy being extravagant at the time, you'll regret it later on when the credit card bill arrives or you get a stiff letter from your bank manager.

JUNE AT A GLANCE

Love	♥ ♥ ♥ ♥
Money	£ $ £ $ £
Career	💻
Health	☼ ☼

• Tuesday 1 June •

Someone is full of talk today and the trouble is that they won't know when to shut up. They might ramble on about all sorts of trivial details, not realizing that you have neither the time nor the inclination to listen to them, especially if you've heard it all before. The temptation will be to get impatient or ratty, but is that really necessary?

• Wednesday 2 June •

Be careful if you're supposed to be saving your money today because it's likely to fly through your fingers in no time at all. You're open to all sorts of delicious impulses now, such as splashing out your hard-earned cash on little treats or great big purchases. Indulgence is the key here, and you'll also want to push the boat out if you're going to a restaurant for a meal. You'll work your way through the menu, regardless of the cost.

• *Thursday 3 June* •

Get involved in financial transactions at your peril today, because certain people will use them as a stick to beat you with. For instance, if you ask someone to lend you money they may either make you feel guilty about it or dredge up all sorts of past instances when their trust was betrayed. You would also be well advised to avoid any show of possessiveness or jealousy, even if you feel it, unless you truly don't care about the disastrous outcome.

• *Friday 4 June* •

Your spirits are high and you're feeling great! It's a super day for doing whatever appeals to you, provided it involves plenty of enjoyment and laughter. The thought of struggling through a pile of work is likely to leave you cold, and you'll be tempted to put it off until you're more in the mood. If you can, visit somewhere new now.

• *Saturday 5 June* •

During the coming fortnight it will be very important for you to think deeply about your current financial situation. Go through paperwork, and make sure you know what's happening and what is being done in your name. If you aren't certain about what to do for the best, make an appointment to see your bank manager or financial adviser, or a clued-up friend.

• Sunday 6 June •

You're in a chatty mood but you won't want to talk about trivia. Instead, you'll relish getting your teeth into some serious topics and showing that you know what you're talking about. It's an especially good day for talking to people who are older or more influential than you, and you'll create a very good impression if that's what you want to happen.

• Monday 7 June •

This is a marvellous day for getting on with the business at hand, whatever that happens to be. You don't want to waste your time on what you see as frivolities, yet you won't want to get bogged down in a lot of serious stuff either. Instead, you want to keep ahead of the game, do your best and be as efficient as possible. All of which you should manage quite easily.

• Tuesday 8 June •

It's a fabulous day for talking about matters connected with money and your general values because you'll find it easy to put across your views without treading on anyone's toes. What's more, you'll be delighted to discover that everyone seems to be thinking along the same lines and you're in general agreement about what is important right now.

• Wednesday 9 June •

Prepare for some shocks and surprises today! You might have to cope with some unexpected events or someone could make a suggestion that leaves you open-mouthed with astonishment. It's not a good day for making decisions connected with your finances because your thoughts are all over the place and you might therefore choose an option that turns out to be more trouble than it's worth.

• *Thursday 10 June* •

You're very fond of you-know-who but you can't help wondering what on earth they're talking about today. They're full of bright ideas and high hopes, but most of these seem to have more to do with wishful thinking than reality, as far as you're concerned. Even so, beware of pouring cold water over all their schemes because you never know, they could be on to a winner with some of them.

• *Friday 11 June* •

You'll have to proceed with great care today if you want to avoid stirring up trouble or opposition. It seems that certain people are feeling very threatened by the prospect of change, and as a result are determined to cling to the status quo no matter what the cost. Do your best to avoid behaving in this way yourself because it won't do you any favours. Be more flexible if possible.

• *Saturday 12 June* •

You're silver-tongued and highly communicative today, so make the most of it while it lasts. Use this opportunity to talk to others about whatever is uppermost in your mind at the moment. You'll be able to put across your ideas with tact and consideration. It's also an excellent day for thinking about your priorities in life and perhaps re-evaluating some of them.

• *Sunday 13 June* •

Let your imagination flow, particularly when thinking about how to advance your career or make progress with long-term goals. However, you'll have to tread a fine line between rising to challenges and knowing your own limitations. Strange as it may seem, daydreaming could be very productive now so take note of the ideas that come to you when your mind wanders.

• *Monday 14 June* •

Efficiency and diligence are your watchwords today, and you want to be as practical and responsible as possible. You'll be perfectly polite when talking to others but you won't want to waste time on anything unnecessary. It's a terrific day for taking part in a discussion or meeting, and your common-sense attitude will win you some admiring glances.

• *Tuesday 15 June* •

So far this month you've had a couple of instances when certain people have refused to adapt to changes and to move with the times, and unfortunately you're faced with another example of this obstinacy today. Even though you might want to scream with frustration, it's no good trying to talk them round because that will make them even more determined to stand their ground. All you can do right now is to respect their decision and leave them to it.

• *Wednesday 16 June* •

Surround yourself with objects and people that give you pleasure! This doesn't have to cost a fortune, even though you'll be tempted to have fun with your chequebook or credit card. For instance, you'd enjoy visiting a local art gallery or museum, or even walking through some beautiful countryside in the company of a special person.

• *Thursday 17 June* •

Today's New Moon is encouraging you to sum up all the thoughts and experiences you've had over the past four weeks and to take some constructive action over them. For instance, if you realize you've got to turn over a new leaf in your finances then you should do so now. Equally, you may need to do something positive about some of your priorities in life.

• *Friday 18 June* •

There's a lot of talk flying around today. The question is whether it's going to achieve anything or whether it will just be an excuse for people to yak away about whatever pops into their heads. Do your best to steer the conversation in sensible directions and not be sidetracked by interesting but unnecessary diversions.

• *Saturday 19 June* •

This is a glorious day for your love life because you're in such a wonderfully expansive and affectionate mood, and so is that special person. So indulge yourselves when you get together and do something special. Maybe this is the perfect excuse to treat yourselves to a romantic dinner in a restaurant, or to have a private celebration at home.

• *Sunday 20 June* •

Oh dear! A certain person is rather hot under the collar today. They're in the sort of mood where they're likely to bite your head off as soon as you open your mouth, so you'd be wise to give them as wide a berth as possible or to choose your words carefully when you're with them. Try not to respond by being equally bad-tempered or touchy: that won't help at all.

• *Monday 21 June* •

During the coming four weeks you'll enjoy getting involved with local issues and neighbourhood concerns. It will be good to feel that you're doing your bit and you'll enjoy knowing what's going on around you. You may be asked to take the lead in some way or to voice your opinion, so don't be shy about putting forward your ideas.

• *Tuesday 22 June* •

You'll fare best today if you can be flexible, especially when plans start to change at the last minute and you're compelled to think on your feet. The more you can go with the flow, the easier everything will be, and you might even start to enjoy not knowing what's round the corner. You might also come up with some radical or futuristic ideas that are well worth pursuing.

• *Wednesday 23 June* •

Between now and early August you'll have a strong desire to devote yourself to your home and family whenever you get the chance. There may be a sense of urgency in all this, perhaps because you've set yourself a deadline and you're determined to meet it, or simply because you want to get certain tasks out of the way as soon as possible. So give it all your best shot.

• *Thursday 24 June* •

A certain person is being touchy and tricky, and you need to handle them with care. They're investing everything with too much importance as far as you're concerned, making them liable to moods and huffs. They may also be feeling sidelined emotionally, and therefore determined to reassert themselves in your affections, even though the method they choose is self-defeating.

• *Friday 25 June* •

If you're worried about what happened yesterday, do your best to discuss it today. You'll find it easy to put your feelings into words without making a big song and dance about things, or expressing them badly. Remember to keep a light touch, to prevent the situation from getting bogged down. Your sense of humour is your greatest ally right now, so use it.

• *Saturday 26 June* •

Hold it! You're moping around as though you've got all the cares of the world on your shoulders and it's making you feel wretched. Your energy may also have drained away, leaving you feeling like a limp rag. So what's wrong? You need to face up to whatever is bugging you and do something about it, otherwise it will continue to dominate your thoughts and ruin your day.

• *Sunday 27 June* •

If you've been unable to shrug off yesterday's downbeat mood, then it's time for some serious action. Try not to keep your worries and feelings to yourself – that will only make them seem worse than ever. Instead, discuss them with someone who is willing to listen and give you some constructive advice. This will help you to put everything in its proper perspective.

• *Monday 28 June* •

Maybe it's reaction to the gloom of the past couple of days but you're feeling restless and easily bored. Ideally, you should abandon at least part of your usual routine and do something radically different instead. Not only will this make you feel more lively, it will also bring you into contact with fresh ideas and new developments which you might otherwise have missed.

• *Tuesday 29 June* •

Financial matters start to get back on track today, and not before time as far as you're concerned. Certain people may also alter their allegiances, making them more sympathetic towards you. This is a good day for keeping abreast of local news, perhaps by having a chat with a neighbour and catching up on all the latest gossip.

• *Wednesday 30 June* •

You're raring to go today, especially when it comes to domestic and family matters. You may even start to feel rather impatient if you suspect that certain people aren't moving as fast as you'd like. It's one thing to chivvy them along but don't bully them. If you've been considering buying items to improve your home, have a look at what's on offer but decide whether you can afford them before taking the plunge and buying them.

JULY AT A GLANCE

Love	♥ ♥ ♥
Money	£ $ £
Career	💻 💻
Health	☼ ☼

• *Thursday 1 July* •

You're in a quiet and meditative mood today, and you're thinking about things very deeply. You may even feel rather impatient or agitated with anyone who wants to focus on the lighter side of life while you'd rather discuss what you consider to be serious issues. Deep and meaningful topics will occupy your thoughts, but don't lose your sense of humour in the process.

• *Friday 2 July* •

Today's Full Moon will be giving you plenty to think about in the next two weeks. What's more, you'll have to view situations from more than one angle in order to work out what's going on, so don't fall into the trap of thinking you've got all the answers in five minutes flat. There's even a chance that you'll be forced to rethink a belief or outlook that you've relied on in the past but which no longer seems such a certainty.

• *Saturday 3 July* •

The planets are emphasizing yesterday's theme by highlighting any situation that calls for careful thought. However, you'll show a tendency to rush into judgements and leap to conclusions, which won't help matters one jot. You should also beware of people who want to show off by appearing to be more clever than they really are. Bear in mind that a lot of what they're saying right now is probably sheer waffle.

• Sunday 4 July •

During the next three weeks your thoughts will never be far from your home and family. Even if you're miles away from them, you'll be doing a lot of thinking about them. If your nearest and dearest are flung far and wide, this is the ideal opportunity to start organizing a reunion or to make contact with some relatives who you haven't spoken to in ages.

• Monday 5 July •

There's no danger of you being assailed by the Monday blues because you're grinning from ear to ear. You're determined to make the best of whatever the day will bring, and it looks as though some very good things are coming your way. For instance, there could be an interesting invitation and you will also have a good laugh with one of your favourite people.

• Tuesday 6 July •

Once again you're wreathed in smiles, which will do wonders for your popularity. It's a super day for taking part in any sort of social activity or group gathering because you'll make a big effort to get on well with everyone you meet. You might end up taking the lead in some way, if only temporarily.

• Wednesday 7 July •

Go carefully today: certain people will soon get themselves into a right old state, especially if they're feeling jealous or possessive. You will also have to guard against slipping into this sort of mood as it will lead to a lot of hassle. If you're annoyed with someone it will be better to say so outright than to convey your message with a moody silence or gigantic sulk.

• *Thursday 8 July* •

You're at your most practical and efficient today, especially if you're writing letters, making phone calls or trying to find out some information. You'll be able to ask sensible questions and will do your best to ensure you're given straightforward answers. If you're talking to a neighbour or close relative, you'll want to stick to the facts and not get sidetracked by gossip or any other sort of irrelevance.

• *Friday 9 July* •

Be careful what you blurt out in the heat of the moment or when you feel vulnerable, because you could accidentally reveal certain facts that you were trying to keep under your hat. Unfortunately, this looks like being a tricky day. Tempers are frayed and you've got a lot of nervous energy that needs a constructive outlet if you want to avoid winding yourself up.

• *Saturday 10 July* •

This is a fantastic day for gathering the family around you and having a mini conference about whatever is important to you all at the moment. For instance, if you're planning on moving house soon, this would be a good opportunity to discuss all the arrangements. However, be prepared for the atmosphere to become slightly heated when talking about certain topics.

• *Sunday 11 July* •

You're very busy today, with plenty to keep you happily occupied. Luckily, you're unlikely to be rushing around like a headless chicken. Instead, you'll be in touch with lots of people or take plenty of short journeys. Today is also a good opportunity to talk to someone who lives nearby, especially if they always have to be humoured in some way.

• Monday 12 July •

Do your best to avoid getting new projects off the ground today as they're likely to go pear-shaped. Things simply won't work out in the way you were hoping, either because they fail to get off the ground in the first place or because they soon become more trouble than they're worth. Instead, concentrate on ventures that are already up and running.

• Tuesday 13 July •

You could be forgiven for thinking that a certain someone doesn't know what they're talking about. Well, that's the impression they're giving, at any rate, because they seem to be making things up as they go along or talking through the back of their head. Be selective about what you believe, and if in doubt check what they're telling you.

• Wednesday 14 July •

It's a good day for keeping in touch with some of your friends and family. You don't have to talk about anything very important – simply making contact with them will be enough to make you feel good. If you're planning a trip to the shops you'll have most fun if you can take someone along to keep you company. Maybe you could find time for a visit to your favourite café?

• Thursday 15 July •

Don't expect the day to go exactly as you were hoping because there could be some changes of plan at some point. Don't worry – these are unlikely to be disruptive or irritating. Instead, they'll simply add a little colour and interest to your schedule. Keep your ear close to the ground: you could hear some fascinating information.

• *Friday 16 July* •

Certain people seem to be going out of their way to trip you up or restrict your progress today, and there won't be much you can do about it. There could be delays that are beyond your control or someone might withdraw their co-operation. Although it will be tempting to tell yourself that this is all part of a major conspiracy, beware of becoming needlessly paranoid or suspicious.

• *Saturday 17 July* •

There's a New Moon today and it's encouraging you to talk about whatever is uppermost in your mind at the moment. Rather than keep your thoughts to yourself it will be far more productive to discuss them either with the people concerned or with anyone who can help you to marshal your thoughts. You might be taking more short journeys than usual during the rest of July.

• *Sunday 18 July* •

This is one of those irritating days in which you should avoid starting any new activities or ventures. They simply won't pan out in the way you want, so you might as well hold your fire for the time being and relax instead. If you're getting together with some of your nearest and dearest today, be prepared for slight hitches that will disrupt the smooth running of your arrangements.

• *Monday 19 July* •

One of the family's in a very chatty mood today, as you'll soon realize when they start talking and barely pause for breath. You'll need the verbal equivalent of a shoehorn if you want to get a word in edgeways, and when you try this and fail you might even get rather ratty. Do your best to avoid getting defensive or huffy. It really isn't worth it.

• Tuesday 20 July •

Red alert! It's one of those days when money flows out of your bank account like a receding tide, and you'll have a whale of a time in the process. Unless you've got iron will-power, you'll be inexorably drawn towards your favourite shops, and once there you'll just have to go on a splurge. As for your love life, some of the delicious events that are lined up will have you dancing on air.

• Wednesday 21 July •

Whenever you possibly can, you should make enjoyment your number one priority today. This shouldn't be difficult because, let's face it, in your present mood you'll do almost anything to avoid unpleasant or boring activities. What's more, you're blessed with enough charm right now to come up with some convincing and tactful excuses if needs be.

• Thursday 22 July •

Between now and late August you'll want to spend a lot of time with familiar people, such as some of your nearest and dearest. You'll feel more comfortable when surrounded by friendly faces than if you're with strangers. This will also be a good opportunity to concentrate on your domestic plans and arrangements, especially if they could do with some improvements or modifications.

• Friday 23 July •

There's a very easy-going atmosphere between you and the people you meet at work today, whether these are bosses, colleagues or customers. You're making a big effort to keep on the right side of everyone you encounter, and you may also make allowances for certain people if they're behaving badly. You could be inspired to improve the appearance of your surroundings at work, even if that only means putting a vase of flowers on your desk.

• *Saturday 24 July* •

If you've got the day off you should try to do as little as possible! Yes, it's one of those days when you're feeling very relaxed and laid-back, and you want to take things gently. So try to find the time for activities that you always enjoy, especially if these involve plenty of food and drink that you can share with some of the special people in your life.

• *Sunday 25 July* •

Financial arrangements are fraught with problems today, including the distinct possibility that someone will pressure you into doing what they want. They could use some very underhand methods in order to bend you to their will, including dropping heavy hints or using emotional blackmail. The green-eyed monster might also cause trouble with a loved one. What a day!

• *Monday 26 July* •

Someone has steam coming out of their ears today, making them difficult to be around. They seem to have worked themselves up into a right old state, especially if you privately consider that they're ranting on about nothing much at all. Mind you, you might decide that it's more than your life is worth to say so, because you'll only get an earful. Keep your head down!

• *Tuesday 27 July* •

There is a strong emphasis on your domestic arrangements at the moment and this is a great day to check that everything is running smoothly. Talking things through with other members of the family will help to keep everyone in the picture and will also give them the opportunity to offer their help if necessary. As a result you'll be delighted to know you've got a strong support system that you can count on when you need it.

• *Wednesday 28 July* •

This is a super day for immersing yourself in your closest and most intimate relationships. So get together with that special person, or with one of your dearest friends, and do your best to make strong emotional connections with them. You'll end up having a greater understanding of one another.

• *Thursday 29 July* •

Keep your mind as active as possible today. You're interested in a wide range of ideas and activities right now, and want to devote as much time to them as possible. If you've got a holiday or long journey coming up, this is a good opportunity to check that all the arrangements are still OK. You could even be inspired to buy a guidebook to your destination so you'll know more about it.

• *Friday 30 July* •

Think twice before being drawn into discussions and philosophical arguments today because they'll soon take a serious turn and then it will be difficult to extricate yourself from them. You may also have to listen to someone who gets on their soapbox and treats you to a lecture. Try not to behave this way yourself, even though it might be strangely tempting.

• *Saturday 31 July* •

It's time to assess the progress of your long-term goals. However, you'll have to be honest with yourself, or the whole thing will be a waste of effort. So evaluate all your current projects to see how they're progressing. If you realize that your heart is no longer in something, it will be far better to jettison it now than to continue with it through fear of what people will say if you abandon it. Do what you know is right and let them say what they like.

AUGUST AT A GLANCE

Love	❤ ❤ ❤ ❤ ❤
Money	£ $ £
Career	💻
Health	☼ ☼ ☼ ☼

• *Sunday 1 August* •

Is there any chance that you-know-who has been taken over by aliens? Weird as that may sound, it seems a distinct possibility right now judging by the strange things they're doing and saying. However, there could be some logic in their actions, even though it's escaping you at the moment. So try to go with the flow, be as open-minded as possible, and not make preconceived judgements about what this person is saying.

• *Monday 2 August* •

Today you're very keen on any activities that will brighten up your life and give you something fresh to think about. As a result, you could become interested in a new hobby that seems to offer you a lot of scope, or you might consider joining a club or organization that's slightly unusual. Some of your ideas may also seem quite radical to you, yet they are worth following up.

• *Tuesday 3 August* •

Put your brain to good use now because you're in a very rational and logical frame of mind. It's a super day for showing how organized and practical you can be, without getting bogged down in details or becoming a stick-in-the-mud. If you get involved in a discussion or negotiation, your intellect and common sense will shine through.

• *Wednesday 4 August* •

A friend needs plenty of attention. That's OK if you can spare the time, but can you? It's highly likely that you've got other claims on your time, in which case you'll have to be very tactful if you're to avoid upsetting this person or making them feel that they aren't important enough to you. You may also receive an invitation that you can't get out of, even if you would like to.

• *Thursday 5 August* •

You're in a nicely sentimental and emotional mood today, without wanting to go overboard or get yourself all worked up. In an ideal world, you should surround yourself with some of your nearest and dearest, or perhaps with one special person, and revel in their company. It's also a super day for luxuriating in your home comforts.

• *Friday 6 August* •

Prepare yourself for what looks like being a difficult day. For a start, you seem riddled with self-doubt and a lack of direction, and this will be exploited by anyone who wants to get the better of you. You're also facing big changes connected with a relationship or financial arrangement, and right now you aren't very keen on the idea. But can you do anything to stop it?

• *Saturday 7 August* •

During the coming four weeks you'll excel at bringing out the best in the people around you. For instance, if a neighbour is usually a total pain in the neck, you may even manage to perform a miracle by appealing to their better nature and keeping them sweet. So make the most of your tact and diplomacy, because they'll be your best friends this month.

• *Sunday 8 August* •

Life is a cabaret today! Well, you may not want to put on the fishnet tights and the bowler hat, but you certainly feel like dancing and singing. What's brought this on? It may be nothing more than a sense of being at one with the world, coupled with a determination to look on the bright side and make the best of whichever cards life has dealt you. When you think about it, what else can you do?

• *Monday 9 August* •

Watch out! You're in a rather combustible mood right now and it won't take much to make you go off bang. What's wrong? You could be feeling got at, especially if a loved one has been nagging you or is being grumpy. There is also a chance that you're subconsciously goading someone into losing their temper so you can have a rip-roaring row with them.

• Tuesday 10 August •

The next six weeks will be a fantastic opportunity to cram as much fun into your life as possible. You'll have a very strong desire to enjoy yourself whenever you get the chance, and that will include making the most of your love life. If you get involved with someone new, the thrill of the chase will be a big part of the fun. Take care, though, not to confuse love with lust.

• Wednesday 11 August •

A local event or neighbourhood activity goes really well today, helped along by your current ability to bring out the best in others. A few well-chosen words could make all the difference to what happens now, and you'll definitely prefer to mollify people than rub them up the wrong way. Remember that if you've got to do something that you aren't looking forward to.

• Thursday 12 August •

The more understanding you can show towards a certain person, the better you'll get on with them now. Even if they're a bit of a mystery and you can't work them out, they'll appreciate the effort you're making to find out what makes them tick. You may never end up being bosom buddies but your present attitude will make them more sympathetic towards you.

• Friday 13 August •

Some of the people in your life are very unpredictable today, and as a result social arrangements could face lots of disruptions. Do your best to go with the flow and see where it takes you, because it could lead you in some highly enjoyable directions. You might also be strongly attracted to someone who isn't normally your cup of tea but who is definitely to your taste right now.

• *Saturday 14 August* •

There are three things you're after today – enjoyment, love and laughter. As a result, you'll want to steer clear of anything that smacks of hard work, drudgery or duty. It's a lovely day for being with some of your favourite people, perhaps sharing a meal or a having a drink together. A trip to a beauty spot or the cinema will also appeal to you now.

• *Sunday 15 August* •

The best way to get on well with someone now is to spend time talking to them. If you can't see them in person, give them a ring or write them a letter so they know you're thinking about them. Any form of discussion will go smoothly now, so it's a good opportunity to bring up topics that could be incendiary if you don't approach them in the right way.

• *Monday 16 August* •

You've been spending a lot of time concentrating on your home and family lately, and today's New Moon is a super opportunity to make any changes or decisions that you think are necessary. For instance, if you've been wondering when to put your house on the market or redesign your garden, it would be a wise move to get the ball rolling within the next two weeks.

• *Tuesday 17 August* •

You're able to combine practicality with creativity today, and that will be a very constructive combination. You stand a good chance of achieving whatever you set out to do, especially if you're relying on other people to give you their support or to co-operate in some way. A relationship will also flourish now, thanks to the effort that you're both putting into it.

• Wednesday 18 August •

A loved one seems to be operating much faster than usual. They may be talking nineteen to the dozen, so that you can barely keep up with what they're saying, and their thought processes have also been speeded up. This will be fun but unfortunately it may also mean that they soon start to get impatient if they think you're lagging behind. Try to keep the atmosphere light-hearted to avoid things degenerating into a row.

• Thursday 19 August •

A friend is prone to some very erratic thinking today, so there's no knowing what they're going to say or do next. You may even suspect that they're taking a perverse delight in keeping you on your toes or being rather contrary. Try not to take what they say as gospel in case they're talking complete nonsense.

• Friday 20 August •

You've got a lot on your plate today and it's getting you down. This could have an impact on your health, making you feel tired or lethargic, and possibly even making you susceptible to any germs that happen to be flying about. If you're really struggling to get everything done in time you may have to ask for help, or accept that you can't work miracles and some-thing's got to give.

• Saturday 21 August •

There's a lot of pleasure to be gained from getting on with domestic and other routine chores today. You'll enjoy gradually ticking them all off your list of things to do, and you'll also take trouble with them so that you do them to the best of your ability. If you can spare the time, you'll enjoy pottering about in the kitchen or throwing out old belongings you no longer need.

• *Sunday 22 August* •

Life will be very pleasant and enjoyable during the next four weeks, with plenty of things to keep you amused. Much to your delight, there will be times when you're the centre of everyone's affection, which will do wonders for your ego. The atmosphere between you and your favourite people will be even sweeter than usual, so there's a lot to look forward to.

• *Monday 23 August* •

There's nothing you'll like better today than having a good old natter with whoever happens to be around. Ideally, you should get together with someone who makes your world go round and then chat away about whatever pops into your head. If you meet someone new now you'll share a relationship in which communications are highlighted for some reason.

• *Tuesday 24 August* •

Still waters run deep today, so even if a loved one isn't saying much it doesn't mean that they're impervious to what's going on around them. You can bet that they're taking it all in, and probably getting into a bit of a state about it. If you suspect that someone is brooding, it's a good idea to encourage them to talk about what's on their mind, even if it makes uncomfortable listening.

• Wednesday 25 August •

Between now and the start of September you should think carefully about any family or domestic plans that are currently in the pipeline. Unforeseen snags could crop up, forcing you to re-evaluate your ideas and possibly even come up with some different solutions. Alternatively, projects may go cold for the time being and you'll just have to be patient.

• Thursday 26 August •

You're in a competitive and adventurous mood today, making you keen to get involved in all sorts of interesting activities. You could even be inspired to do something for the first time, especially if it presents you with a bit of a challenge. Although you'll enjoy feeling the adrenalin racing around your veins, don't do anything totally rash or foolhardy.

• Friday 27 August •

If you get fed up with being thought of as a placid or pragmatic Taurean, you'll jump at the chance to show a different side to your personality today. In fact, the more you suspect that you've been put into a pigeon-hole by other people, the more you'll want to do things that make them sit up and take notice. It's a question of how outrageous you dare to be!

• Saturday 28 August •

Be careful today because your emotions are in a state of flux, which could lead to confusion and mixed messages. You should be especially aware of this when dealing with people of power or influence, in case you give them the wrong impression. It will also be difficult to keep track of your thoughts, so you'll appear to be absent-minded or distracted.

• *Sunday 29 August* •

This is a good day for getting together with some of the family because you'll enjoy one another's company. However, someone could get their knickers in a twist, which will lead to a tricky atmosphere and possibly even some raised voices. This is especially likely if the conversation strays into memories of the past, with people arguing about what really happened.

• *Monday 30 August* •

Strange things could happen with a friend during the next two weeks, giving you an entirely new perspective on them. You might decide that you need to have a word in their ear about something, particularly if you don't want it to happen again. Or you could realize that your feelings for them are changing and you need to do something about it.

• *Tuesday 31 August* •

It's a tricky day, so be careful. You're in need of company but the people you seek out won't have as much time for you as you'd like. They may be genuinely busy with other things, but if you aren't careful you'll convince yourself that they're making excuses because they don't really want to see you. Try not to believe that you've been given the brush-off unless the evidence is overwhelming.

SEPTEMBER AT A GLANCE

Love	♥ ♥ ♥ ♥ ♥
Money	£ $
Career	💻 💻 💻 💻 💻
Health	☼ ☼ ☼ ☼ ☼

• Wednesday 1 September •

Make an effort to get on well with older friends and relatives today, especially if they can sometimes be slightly tricky. You shouldn't have any problems with them right now, particularly if you go out of your way to understand their point of view and listen to what they're saying. If you offer to do them a favour or help them out in some way, then so much the better.

• Thursday 2 September •

During the past few days it hasn't been easy to get going on domestic arrangements and decisions because so much has been out of your hands or just hanging in the balance. But all that should start to change from today, thank goodness, and you'll begin to make progress again. In the meantime, celebrate by doing something enjoyable with some of your favourite people: it's exactly what you're in the mood for.

• Friday 3 September •

This is another super day for placing the emphasis on enjoyment and fun whenever possible. You're in a very light-hearted mood right now and this will rub off on most of the people you meet. If you've currently got high hopes that your relationship with you-know-who will develop into something wonderful, what happens now will have you jumping for joy.

• *Saturday 4 September* •

You're raring to go and keen to be as active as possible today. It's the sort of day when you're easily bored so you'll need plenty of distractions to keep you busy. It's a great day for doing something sporty or athletic, especially if you're being competitive in the process. Naturally, you'll want to win!

• *Sunday 5 September* •

Let's face it, people aren't always going to be as accommodating and flexible as they are at the moment, so if you're wise you'll make the most of it. Do your best to butter up anyone who needs the soft soap treatment – a little tact will go a long way now. How about inviting a neighbour round for a drink or making an effort to talk to them, even if they aren't exactly your favourite person?

• *Monday 6 September* •

During the next few weeks you'll enjoy putting your artistic talents to good use around your home. Maybe the place could do with a facelift, in which case you'll soon come up with some inspirational ideas. Or perhaps something less drastic is needed, such as rearranging the furniture, changing the ornaments, or cleaning the curtains.

• *Tuesday 7 September* •

It's one of those days when you've got to be strict with yourself about your spending, or you could end up parting with more money than you bargained for. You know the sort of thing that can happen – you see something you'd like to buy, then you can't decide which colour to get and so you end up splashing out on one in every colour you fancy. Not good news!

• *Wednesday 8 September* •

Get ready to hear some surprising news today. Someone might drop a mini bombshell or you could discover that a forth-coming social arrangement has got to be rejigged. Rather than fret and fume about all this, it will be much simpler to take it in your stride and wait to see what happens next. If you think about it, you don't really have much choice, do you?

• *Thursday 9 September* •

Your powers of attraction are ace today, so turn them to your advantage. If you're hoping to ensnare a certain someone and convince them that you're the best thing since chocolate ice cream, give it your best shot right now. If they still resist you after you've turned on the charm like a waterfall, they don't deserve you and you're better off without them.

• *Friday 10 September* •

The next few weeks are perfect for giving your brain some enjoyable exercise. That could mean burying your nose in a succession of books and only coming out for food, or you might fancy your chances with competitions, puzzles and pub quizzes. It will be a great time for mixing with children, and you'll enjoy playing with them or going on an adventure together.

• *Saturday 11 September* •

Doublecheck everything if you're filling in forms, writing important letters or doing anything else connected with red tape today. That's because your mind won't really be on the job and, as a result, you could make some silly mistakes that you'll kick yourself about when you discover them later on. It won't help if someone is subtly trying to undermine you, either.

• *Sunday 12 September* •

A battle of wills is more than likely today, especially if changes are in the air and someone is fiercely resisting them. Such determination to prevent these changes will be about as much use as trying to stem the tide with a handkerchief but that won't deter this person from stubbornly sticking to their guns and refusing to accept the inevitable. Don't behave like this yourself or you'll face a lot of opposition and hassle.

• *Monday 13 September* •

There have been several occasions recently when you've had cause to doubt the sanity of a certain person because they're behaving so eccentrically, and this is another day when you can only marvel at their erratic and contrary goings-on. Should you play these down or make a big thing out of them? Bear in mind that your protests are likely to encourage this person to act even more weirdly, so you may be shooting yourself in the foot.

• *Tuesday 14 September* •

Today's New Moon will bring good news about loved ones during the next two weeks. You could hear about the imminent arrival of a baby, receive an invitation to a party or wedding, or have some other reason for breaking open the champagne and getting out your best clothes. If a love affair gets off the ground now it will make your heart sing with happiness. Aaaah!

• *Wednesday 15 September* •

Today you'll encounter someone who is very special to you but who's being rather domineering or overwhelming at the moment. You love them but you can't help wishing they'd tone down their personality for a short while because they're showing a tendency to go over the top. All the same, you won't want to dampen their high spirits or spoil their day.

• Thursday 16 September •

If you're at work someone will be very kind to you. For instance, a colleague might look out for you in some way or a customer could show how much they appreciate all your efforts. If you're expected to be ruthless or tough today, it will be a struggle to pull this off because your instincts are telling you to be considerate and placatory. You want to be nice, not nasty!

• Friday 17 September •

This is a good day for sorting out any situations that are threatening to wreak havoc or grind to a halt. You're brimming with common sense right now and it shows! You'll want to do whatever is the most sensible and practical option, and this will probably involve talking to other people to find out what's going on. Make sure you've got all the facts straight first.

• Saturday 18 September •

Deception is in the air today, so be careful. Someone may be trying to pull the wool over your eyes or perhaps you're capable of doing it to yourself. Your behaviour is in marked contrast to yesterday, because you're now in a world of your own and when faced with any unpleasant facts will want to bury your head in the sand and completely ignore them. But is that sensible?

• *Sunday 19 September* •

Once again you're very diplomatic and tactful today, which is just what you want if you're hoping to win someone over to your side or get them to understand what you're talking about. If you've got to break the ice with someone, you'll manage to do it now and, with luck, the temperature between you will quickly become warmer. If it doesn't, it's unlikely to be through any fault of your own.

• *Monday 20 September* •

During the past few days you've managed to say exactly the right thing at the right time, which makes what happens today even more frustrating than it would be normally. Instead of being able to choose your words carefully, you're suddenly struggling to keep out of verbal trouble, particularly if someone close to your heart upsets you or makes you feel threatened. You'll say something sharp or unfortunate without even being aware of what you're doing.

• *Tuesday 21 September* •

You're in a marvellously expansive and happy mood today, and you want everyone around you to share your current sense of bonhomie. You can't help viewing life from a highly optimistic angle. It looks as though this will be completely justified when it comes to your love life, because someone special is going to make your day, if not your week, or even your entire month if you're really lucky.

• *Wednesday 22 September* •

You've been eager to enjoy yourself as much as possible during the past four weeks but from today the emphasis shifts to your work and obligations. So you must now be prepared to reduce the amount of time you spend playing and increase the amount of work you do. If you know that you need to make adjustments to your working life, start as you mean to go on.

• *Thursday 23 September* •

This is a terrific day for getting on with the job in hand, whatever that might be. You're in an efficient and businesslike frame of mind, and this will come across loud and clear to anyone who happens to be around you. You'll shine if you're taking part in a meeting or interview, and you might also get the chance to boost your reputation as a result of the way you deal with others.

• *Friday 24 September* •

It's time to introduce some creative and positive changes into some of your emotional relationships. For instance, you might realize that you need to take a different tack with a relative in order to improve the atmosphere between you, or you could reach an important turning point with your lover. The key to this is to behave in ways that will enhance the situation and benefit both of you, rather than simply to go for the option that works solely for you.

• *Saturday 25 September* •

From today you're being encouraged to pay more attention to your health and general well-being, and this situation will continue throughout the rest of the year. You might decide to increase the amount of exercise you take every day, or adopt a health regime that's designed to lead to the birth of a brand-new you. Try to avoid too much rich food because it won't agree with you.

• *Sunday 26 September* •

This is a fantastic day for putting your thoughts into words or getting them down on paper. Your ideas are well organized, you're thinking clearly, and you know what you want to say. It's a great day for having an important conversation with a loved one, as a result of which you're both able to put across your point of view and reach some sort of compromise.

• *Monday 27 September* •

You're blessed with abundant energy and vitality today, which is fabulous. You don't want to sit still and you're hatching some ambitious plans about what you're going to achieve in the course of the day. That's terrific, but do your best to pace yourself – otherwise you'll run out of steam halfway through a difficult project or, even worse, end up pulling a muscle. So be sensible!

• *Tuesday 28 September* •

What's worrying you? Come on, you know that something is, and you aren't going to feel better until you've taken some concrete action. The more you dither or push it to the back of your mind, the more it will haunt you and drain your energy. So take a deep breath, stare it straight in the face and do whatever will alleviate the problem and make life easier for you.

• *Wednesday 29 September* •

You're thinking and talking big today, and you don't want to put any limit on your imagination. That's perfect if you're normally rather hidebound and reserved, because you'll benefit from pushing yourself further than normal. But if you already have a tendency to hatch overblown or over-ambitious plans, you might get really carried away now and develop strategies that haven't a hope of ever seeing the light of day. So know your limitations and then you'll do really well.

• Thursday 30 September •

Friends are interesting company now and they'll give you plenty to think about. One chum might make some suggestions that seem rather daring or outrageous but which definitely appeal to you. Well, maybe you should give them a try and see what happens next? If you can find the time, you'll enjoy taking part in a group activity or getting to grips with a favourite hobby.

OCTOBER AT A GLANCE

Love	♥ ♥ ♥ ♥ ♥
Money	£
Career	💻 💻 💻 💻 💻
Health	☼ ☼ ☼ ☼ ☼

• Friday 1 October •

Your thoughts are wandering in several directions at once today, which is bad news if you're supposed to be concentrating on something important or official. Trying to pin down your thoughts will be about as easy as catching a bar of soap in the bath – they'll keep slipping out of your grasp. If necessary, get someone else to check what you've done or postpone the whole thing until you're more in the mood to tackle it.

• Saturday 2 October •

Family gatherings are enjoyable right now, provided everyone knows how to behave themselves and keep a tight lid on their feelings. However, if anyone allows themselves to get upset you'll have quite a task on your hands to maintain the status quo. It's a super day for giving your home some attractive decorative touches, and they don't have to cost a fortune, either.

• Sunday 3 October •

Love will brighten up your world this month and will arrive in many different guises. There will be some wonderful encounters with a few of your favourite people, or just one in particular. If you've been wondering when Cupid would strike, get ready to feel the effect of his arrows any day now. Even if you don't fall in love with someone you'll still receive plenty of affection from others, and you'll want to give it in return.

• Monday 4 October •

Matters connected with money, values and sex have a knack of getting under your skin today, so you'll take them a lot more seriously than usual. You'll also be taking yourself more seriously than normal, which could lead to some sticky scenes because of your refusal to be flexible or allow others to dictate terms. You may want to stand your ground, but how far should you take this?

• Tuesday 5 October •

You're in the perfect position to tackle paperwork, filing and any other tasks that need you to be at your most efficient. It's also a super day for inventing systems that will help you to be more practical or businesslike in the future. However, you won't get much done if you give in to the temptation to yak your head off with colleagues. Keep work and play separate!

• *Wednesday 6 October* •

The success or otherwise of today all depends on how willing you are to go with the flow and allow others to be free spirits. If you want to control everything that's happening around you, or restrict a loved one's freedom, you'll soon discover that you're on a collision course with trouble. So grit your teeth and accept that you can't own someone's heart – they must give it to you willingly.

• *Thursday 7 October* •

You're excellent at formulating ideas and making your brain work overtime today, and you'll be delighted by the sharpness and incisiveness of your thinking. Some people may accuse you of being rather tough or unsentimental, but right now you know that you have to deal with the facts of the matter, even though they may be quite unpleasant.

• *Friday 8 October* •

Someone is expecting far too much from you today. They seem to think that you should be sacrificing yourself on their behalf in some way, and this is throwing up difficult problems. You are perfectly happy to help them but you don't want to give the impression that you're being a doormat. There may also be some discrepancy in your status, which is adding to the current difficulties.

• *Saturday 9 October* •

You're very keen to get to the bottom of situations today, especially if you suspect that some sort of mystery surrounds them. Although you'll stop short of giving anyone the third degree, nevertheless you'll want to extract the truth from them and you won't be amused if you suspect they're shilly-shallying or keeping something from you.

• *Sunday 10 October* •

Want to do yourself a favour? Then surround yourself with some of your favourite people, because it will do your soul good to spend time with them. You don't have to do anything very ambitious together, either, so simply sharing a meal or having a gentle chat will keep you perfectly happy. You'll also get a big kick out of doing something creative at some point.

• *Monday 11 October* •

The emotional temperature rises by several degrees today, leading to some hot and heavy scenes. It's one of those days when things take on more significance than usual, making you prone to losing your temper or getting your knickers in a twist. This is especially likely if the antics of a loved one arouse your innate possessiveness or jealousy. Try to play it all down.

• *Tuesday 12 October* •

Are you on a diet or healthy eating regime at the moment? If so, you'd better padlock the fridge, throw away the chocolate and banish the alcohol, because this is one of those days when your will-power is as fragile as a snowflake and just as likely to melt away. Unless it's essential that you stick to your usual sensible diet, it's probably best if you give yourself a couple of little treats and then stop. Otherwise you're likely to resist temptation for only so long before going on a binge.

• *Wednesday 13 October* •

Someone is being overly critical and sharp today, or so it seems to you. You're getting the distinct impression that you can't do anything right and that you're being a complete klutz. You may also start to doubt your mental abilities, perhaps telling yourself that you're not as clever as you imagine or that you can't measure up to what's expected of you. But how true is this? Maybe you're simply being paranoid and lacking in confidence?

• *Thursday 14 October* •

Today's eclipsed New Moon is sending you a powerful message about the importance of taking care of your health over the coming fortnight. It's the ideal opportunity to embark on a new eating plan, to take more exercise, or to give yourself a detox. If you want to get into svelte shape for Christmas, you should start now and take full advantage of the power of the New Moon.

• *Friday 15 October* •

The best way to understand other people right now is to talk to them. And if that doesn't get you very far, you must be prepared to talk to them again until you're both speaking the same language and you have a full understanding of each other. The rest of the month is perfect for taking part in negotiations or discussions, and also for simply listening to what others are telling you.

• *Saturday 16 October* •

You're very organized and together this Saturday, which is fantastic for making things happen or talking about important topics. You have no desire to waste time on trivialities, so you'll want to cut to the chase as soon as possible. Needless to say, you have some important points to make and you'll earn a lot of respect as a result.

• *Sunday 17 October* •

You need to keep an open mind now in order to get the most out of the day. Friends and partners are saying or doing things that will make you raise your eyebrows in surprise. Although your initial instinct may be to reject what you're seeing or hearing as too avant-garde, controversial or challenging, you'll soon change your mind and find it quite exciting.

• *Monday 18 October* •

Pay attention to your finances today by making sure that they're ticking over OK. If a bill has got to be paid within the next few days it's a good idea to get it out of the way now in case you forget about it later on. If there has been a query about the amount of money you earn, or the amount you've got to pay in tax, this is a good opportunity to get to grips with the whole tedious business.

• *Tuesday 19 October* •

Someone is in an expansive mood today and it's good to be around them. They're full of fun and laughter, so their company is almost guaranteed to make you feel good. But you should take what they're saying with a pinch of salt because it's highly likely that they're spouting exaggerated claims or making promises that they can't keep. If you believe them, you could be disappointed later on.

• *Wednesday 20 October* •

Tread very carefully in all emotional matters today because they're like a minefield. Someone is being very resistant to any hint of change in your relationship, and unfortunately the more threatened they feel, the more they'll resist what is being proposed. There could also be some jealous scenes even if these aren't warranted, so be careful not to provoke anyone unnecessarily.

• *Thursday 21 October* •

It's easy for people to speak out of turn today, especially if they think they've got the upper hand for some reason. For instance, someone in a high position may let their power go to their head a little, making them rather bossy or arrogant. You could also get caught up in an argument over petty details, so the whole thing gets out of hand. Try not to let this happen.

• *Friday 22 October* •

You've got plenty of energy to channel into your work, and as a result you'll enjoy doing everything to the best of your ability. This is great if you've been trying to summon up the energy to do something tedious or rather difficult, because you'll happily wade right in now and do your best. Today is also a good day for sorting out problems with colleagues by being straightforward.

• *Saturday 23 October* •

You'll excel at any form of team work during the next four weeks, and it will definitely be a time when you're happiest if you can be with other people. You'll also get a strong sense that your own identity is tied up with that of the people in your life, and you may want to give them more power or authority over you than usual.

• *Sunday 24 October* •

The more sociable you can be today, the happier you'll feel. It's not a day to lock yourself away and not see a soul, unless you don't have any choice in the matter. Friends and acquaintances are good fun and will bring out the best in you. If you're taking part in a group gathering, you'll want to do your bit to make sure it all goes well. You may even take the lead at some point.

• *Monday 25 October* •

The best way to relax right now is to do things that you always enjoy and to be with people who lift your spirits. You're in the mood to channel as much energy as possible into your relationships, and you'll expect the same in return from the people you're with. If they fail to live up to your expectations you'll be disappointed and possibly even rather miffed. But don't blow things out of proportion.

• *Tuesday 26 October* •

This is a wonderful day for letting someone know that you care about them. You won't want to do this in a very upfront or obvious way, so you'll be quite subtle about it. You might even let your actions speak louder than words, but even then you won't be over the top. Don't worry about not getting your message across – you'll be sending it in exactly the right way.

• *Wednesday 27 October* •

If there is something that needs sorting out, you'll be on the case today. You won't want to muck about, either, and will be quite direct about what's wrong. It's an especially good day for getting to grips with official money matters or health problems, particularly if you've been feeling anxious about them for some reason.

• *Thursday 28 October* •

Today's eclipsed Full Moon will have a very powerful impact on your personal life during the next couple of weeks. It's telling you to cut out the dead wood from your world, even if this means being quite ruthless or facing up to some unpalatable facts. If you don't make these changes yourself, you'll find that fate takes a hand and does it for you, and this may not be so easy to cope with.

● *Friday 29 October* ●

During the next few weeks you'll do your utmost to deliver service with a smile. You'll take pride in doing your best at work, and also in maintaining as harmonious a relationship as possible with your colleagues and customers. If you've got the hots for a workmate, things could really start to happen now, so be prepared to be swept off your feet.

● *Saturday 30 October* ●

Money is burning a hole in your pocket today, especially if you've just been paid or you've got a lot of cash on you. Be strict with yourself about what you buy, otherwise you'll find that you've frittered away a lot more than you thought. If you're going food shopping you'll be tempted to treat yourself to all sorts of edible luxuries, whether you can afford them or not.

● *Sunday 31 October* ●

Someone needs to calm down! They're taking everything far too seriously and have long since lost their sense of humour. You may have to treat them like an unexploded bomb because you're frightened of them blowing up in your face. They may also be using some form of emotional blackmail in order to make you do what they want. Resist the temptation to give as good as you get.

NOVEMBER AT A GLANCE

Love	♥ ♥ ♥ ♥ ♥
Money	£ $ £ $ £
Career	💻 💻 💻 💻
Health	☼ ☼ ☼ ☼

• Monday 1 November •

Don't expect everything to go according to plan today. Although it's highly unlikely that all your arrangements will unravel before your very eyes, nevertheless you should be prepared for some last-minute changes to take place. You'll have to think on your feet, and also give up any idea that you can control your environment because, right now, you can't.

• Tuesday 2 November •

Some straight talking is called for and you're just the person to do it. You won't want to subject anyone to a ticking-off unless it's absolutely necessary, but nevertheless you'll be speaking straight from the shoulder and you won't be mincing your words. This is a marvellous day for taking part in a negotiation or discussion because your mind is as sharp as a razor.

• Wednesday 3 November •

More haste, less speed! You're trying to do far too much in far too short a time, and all you'll achieve will be to go round in circles or get yourself into a total mess. So calm down, take a deep breath and do things one at a time. If you're in too much of a hurry you'll either make a hash of everything and have to start again, or you'll end up in a furious temper and completely at odds with the rest of the world.

• *Thursday 4 November* •

Be careful, because it seems that someone is doing their best to undermine you in subtle but profound ways. There may even be some sort of treachery afoot, and you should certainly be very careful about who you trust. But you must also be careful not to send out confusing messages yourself, because these could easily be misinterpreted, leading to recriminations later on.

• *Friday 5 November* •

If you're celebrating Bonfire Night, or having a belated Hallowe'en party, you couldn't have chosen a better day to whoop it up. You're in the mood to cast caution to the winds and indulge yourself with plenty of delicious food and drink. This might also be a red-letter day on the work front, giving you good reason to raise a glass and toast your own good fortune.

• *Saturday 6 November* •

If you're a typical Taurean you like to know where you stand. But that isn't the way things are today, particularly when dealing with loved ones and friends. In fact, certain people seem to be going out of their way to shock you, do the opposite of what you suggest, and generally try your patience to the limit. There's nothing you can do about this except go with the flow. But can you?

• *Sunday 7 November* •

This is a wonderful day for getting together with friends and dear ones. You'll relish the chance to spend some time with them, especially if you're all doing something light-hearted together. You could also hear something nice that massages your ego and reminds you yet again that you are loved by many different people. Sometimes life can be very sweet!

• *Monday 8 November* •

This is a super day for tucking someone under your wing and taking care of them, particularly if they're feeling vulnerable in some way. For instance, if someone isn't very well you'll want to do your Florence Nightingale act on them, even if they're breathing germs all over you. There might also be some delicious romantic developments between you and a colleague.

• *Tuesday 9 November* •

It's another day when you're happy to lend a hand wherever it's needed, without any thought for what you might expect in return. Do your best to show compassion and understanding to the people around you, even if you struggle to tolerate them sometimes. Right now, you're prepared to give them the benefit of the doubt and not expect too much from them.

• *Wednesday 10 November* •

A certain person is being very cutting today, particularly if they think you're letting the side down in some way or not pulling your weight. Before you develop a total inferiority complex about this, you should realize that this person is probably being completely unreasonable and also that picking on you is a rather unhelpful way to boost their own faltering ego. Be kind to them and see if that makes a difference to their attitude.

• *Thursday 11 November* •

During the next few weeks you'll feel a strong urge to channel your energy into your relationships. You'll want them to be as successful as possible and you'll do your best to make this happen. However, you'll soon get rather ratty if you suspect that other people don't share your current aims, and you'll also be annoyed if they fail to agree with you on certain points. Be more tolerant!

• *Friday 12 November* •

Today's New Moon will be highlighting your relationships during the rest of the month. It's a fantastic opportunity to make a commitment to someone, such as moving in with them, getting married or embarking on a business venture together. You may also want to adopt a new strategy with a certain person in order to improve the atmosphere between you.

• *Saturday 13 November* •

Your imagination is your best friend right now because it's allowing you to come up with some fabulous ideas and concepts. What's more, it's working in ways that you wouldn't normally expect by guiding you into making the right decisions about your finances and long-term goals. It will also help to discuss these with a sympathetic listener.

• *Sunday 14 November* •

You're easily swayed by your emotions today, and there may even be times when you abandon rationality and follow your heart instead. Even so, it seems that you'll have to be very clever about knowing what you can say and what is better left unsaid at the moment. You shouldn't stay completely silent but you're in danger of saying too much.

• *Monday 15 November* •

The dynamic personality of you-know-who gives you a massive shot of energy and adrenalin today, making you feel on top of the world. It might be your other half who gives you this life-enhancing boost or it could be a friend, but either way they'll open your eyes to all sorts of exciting possibilities that you hadn't considered until now. Come on, Taurus, live a little!

• Tuesday 16 November •

Devote part of today to getting in touch with far-flung friends and family. Give them a ring, send them an e-mail, or arrange to see them as soon as possible. You might even be inspired to invite them to stay with you in the near future. Today's also a good day for getting together with people from different walks of life – you'll enjoy learning more about the world from them.

• Wednesday 17 November •

Someone is being a right old grump today. They're in a bad mood and it seems that they're perfectly happy to stay that way because it gives them the excuse to shout, stamp their feet and generally be a pain in the neck. The question is whether their behaviour has anything to do with you. You may not think so but perhaps you're unconsciously winding them up in some way?

• Thursday 18 November •

If your job requires you to be tough or issue orders, your heart simply won't be in it today. Instead, you'd prefer to take a softly-softly approach in which you consider other people's needs and back off when necessary. So how are you going to reconcile this dilemma? You may have to be sneaky about it, but don't leave yourself open to accusations of having double standards.

• *Friday 19 November* •

Get ready for a major clash between you and a certain person today. The more it's been brewing lately, the bigger the fallout is likely to be. Even though you may be feeling deeply annoyed by what happens now, it's important that you don't make it worse by letting your temper get the better of you and saying or doing things that you'll regret when you've calmed down.

• *Saturday 20 November* •

You need to develop a tough shell today because there's a rather chilly atmosphere and it's got nothing to do with the weather. It seems that someone is being distant or unfriendly, and you'll probably imagine that it's because they've gone off you. It's more likely that they're busy with other things, unless this is all part of a long-running saga in which they're giving you the cold shoulder. If so, you may want to end things between you now.

• *Sunday 21 November* •

The next four weeks are the ideal time to immerse yourself in your most intimate and close relationships. Make a big effort to analyse why you are involved in the way you are, and what you can learn from the situation. The more honest you are with yourself about this, the more productive the experience will be. So look deeply into yourself.

• *Monday 22 November* •

The emphasis is on partnerships right now, and they become even more important to you from today. During the next few weeks you'll want to do your utmost to ensure that partners are happy, and also to prevent any chance of them getting annoyed with you. However, try to resist a tendency to put your own needs second if it would be far better to say what you want upfront.

• *Tuesday 23 November* •

This is a good day to keep a weather eye on your finances and to ensure that everything is going well. For instance, you might want to balance your chequebook or go through a credit card statement. It's also a good idea to do some research into any investments or major outlays that you're considering at the moment, such as a mortgage or pension plan.

• *Wednesday 24 November* •

You're feeling drawn to people who are chalk to your cheese, so don't be surprised if you experience a strong attraction to someone who isn't usually your cup of tea. If a new relationship gets off the ground now it will be unusual in some way and will bring out aspects of your personality that are normally kept hidden. It's going to be very exciting!

• *Thursday 25 November* •

You aren't very sure of yourself today, but be careful about who knows it. They might try to take advantage of your current uncertainty, perhaps by doing you down in some way or simply by putting you on the defensive. There could also be confusion about someone's instructions, with you not understanding what they're talking about. If so, ask them to be clearer.

• *Friday 26 November* •

It's important that you take care of your money during the next two weeks, and also that you keep a strict eye on your spending. If you're wondering how you're going to be able to afford to buy all those Christmas presents on your list you may have to introduce an economy drive or make other contingency plans. What you can't do is bury your head in the sand and pretend it's not happening because that will lead to more problems in the end.

• *Saturday 27 November* •

Grab the chance to pamper yourself in some way today. You know you want to! You'll be drawn to items that are natural rather than man-made, such as clothes made from silk or wool. You'll also enjoy using oils, perfumes and other unguents that make you feel or smell good, but don't overdo them or you could end up feeling slightly sick.

• *Sunday 28 November* •

Your values clash with those of a loved one today, and unless you're very careful the result will be verbal fisticuffs. If this happens, you'll end up having one of those nit-picking rows in which each of you details all the transgressions that the other one has committed lately, so you go round in circles and get increasingly angry. Isn't there a better way than this?

• *Monday 29 November* •

Think big! You're capable of making some important and far-reaching changes to your long-term goals today, provided you have the necessary vision and self-belief, although you won't get anywhere if you indulge in ridiculous fantasies that haven't a hope of coming true. Nor should you restrict yourself to modest plans if you know full well that you're capable of achieving so much more. So be prepared to dream a little.

• *Tuesday 30 November* •

This looks like being a very frustrating day in which you're stymied by someone's inertia or lack of enthusiasm. They may even try to sabotage your plans in some way, although you may not realize this at first because they're being so subtle about it. Make sure you don't add to the problems by underestimating your own abilities or allowing yourself to be demoralized.

DECEMBER AT A GLANCE

Love	♥ ♥ ♥
Money	£ $ £ $ £
Career	💻 💻
Health	☼ ☼

• *Wednesday 1 December* •

Your mind is working really well today, so it's a great opportunity to get ahead with your Christmas preparations. Any form of writing suits you down to the ground now, so how about finishing off your Christmas cards if you haven't yet done so? And if you haven't even started them then make an effort to begin now and you'll find that things go like clockwork.

• *Thursday 2 December* •

This is a day for turning your attention to your finances, especially if you're currently trying to devise the budget for some domestic improvements or changes. Talk to the other people concerned and really listen to what they're saying because they'll have some great insights. It will be far more productive to work as part of a harmonious team than as warring factions.

• Friday 3 December •

Someone simply isn't being realistic or practical today. They seem to be lost in a dream world of wishful thinking and idealism, none of which has anything to do with what's really going on. Unfortunately, they won't want to hear any of this and may even manipulate the situation so they don't have to listen to your opinions. Be careful when dealing with them and try not to get sucked into their current desire to escape reality at all costs.

• Saturday 4 December •

If you gave up in despair over what happened yesterday, you stand a better chance of sorting things out today. Talking to the person concerned may help them to get a grip on the situation, especially if you manage to avoid recriminations or accusations. Instead, do your best to be as understanding and compassionate as possible.

• Sunday 5 December •

There are powerful forces at work in a relationship today, and they'll have quite an impact on you. If you're with that special person in your life, don't be surprised if there's a lot of sexual tension between you that manifests as irritation and bad temper. You'll probably have a huge row and then have a very enjoyable time making up!

• Monday 6 December •

This is another day on which you should be monitoring the progress you've made so far with the festivities and deciding what has still to be done. You're operating very efficiently right now but you'll be even more effective if you can plan your time carefully, write lists of what you must buy or make, and be realistic about your capabilities. But don't expect to work miracles.

• *Tuesday 7 December* •

You have a strong urge to get to the bottom of any mystery that you're currently faced with, whether it involves a personal relationship, a hunch about what's happening or a financial situation. What's more, you won't be satisfied until you've completely solved the puzzle. However, you'll only arouse bad feeling if you pry into things that are none of your business, so beware!

• *Wednesday 8 December* •

Social situations bring out the best in you right now, especially if they encourage you to be a free spirit and you don't have to worry about being on your best behaviour all the time. In fact, you'll welcome the chance to kick over the traces in some way or to remind certain people that you're a much more complex personality than they sometimes give you credit for.

• *Thursday 9 December* •

There's a certain amount of friction between you and partners today. This could be really exciting and dynamic, spurring you into fresh adventures together, or it might lead to spats that seem to get more petty as the day wears on. So resist the temptation to get drawn in to silly squabbles and instead try to express today's energy in more positive ways.

• *Friday 10 December* •

You're in a very analytical mood today and you'll enjoy looking deeply at any situation that you're currently involved in. Ideally, you should have a far-reaching conversation with someone you trust, in which you're both able to say what's on your mind. You might also enjoy reading a psychotherapy or self-help book about some of the issues you're facing right now.

• *Saturday 11 December* •

Whistle while you work! You're keen to enjoy yourself whenever possible, and you don't see why you should have a long face while doing the chores. So switch on the radio or CD player, make your surroundings as amenable as possible and devote yourself to the task in hand as though it were your most favourite occupation in the whole world. What a difference this will make!

• *Sunday 12 December* •

Today's New Moon is focused on your most private and intimate relationships and is encouraging you to make a fresh effort with them. For instance, if your sex life has become rather jaded recently, this is a great opportunity to spice it up. You might also embark on a new alliance now, in which case it will be intense and there may even be a fated quality to it. Sounds interesting!

• *Monday 13 December* •

You're feeling very constructive today and this will impress the people around you. If you're trying to sort out a problem with someone, it should be a piece of cake now because you'll be able to combine a level-headed approach with a desire for harmony and co-operation. You will also get the chance to forge a greater understanding with a certain person, which is all to the good.

• *Tuesday 14 December* •

Are you in listening mode today? Let's hope so, because someone wants to bend your ear and they're hoping that you can spare the time and energy for them. Although your first instincts may tell you to give them plenty of advice, try to stop yourself volunteering it unless it's asked for. Even then, you may get the sense that you're really being asked to listen, not talk.

• *Wednesday 15 December* •

Catch up with the chores today, especially if you've got a list of them as long as your arm and you want to get through them all before Christmas. You're feeling nicely efficient without wanting to work yourself into the ground, so carry on at a steady pace. A few well-chosen words in a certain person's ear will be more effective than a lengthy conversation at other times.

• *Thursday 16 December* •

During the rest of the month you'll enjoy being with people who know you inside out, and with whom you share a strong bond. You'll also want to be more forthcoming and emotional than usual, and may find yourself getting involved in heartfelt conversations and really intense exchanges. At times you may feel slightly exposed but it's important for you to open up emotionally right now.

• Friday 17 December •

Someone is being very short-tempered, and they're liable to fly off the handle at a moment's notice. Maybe they're feeling vulnerable in some way or are desperately trying to defend what they see as their territory. Be sensitive to this and don't goad them into being even more irritable or upset than they are already. Frankly, it's just not worth it.

• Saturday 18 December •

It's another day when emotional tension makes you feel as though you're tiptoeing around on eggshells. However, it seems that the temperature has risen by several degrees, making the situation more fraught than it was yesterday. It will be better to clear the air quickly and cleanly than to sulk and brood in ways that simply prolong the agony.

• Sunday 19 December •

A significant person in your life is a law unto themselves today, and it's driving you crazy! They may withdraw from you in some way or hint that they need more freedom in your relationship. However, clinging on to this person is not the answer right now. You might also be powerfully attracted to someone who's off limits or bad news, yet it seems you can't help yourself.

• Monday 20 December •

You've faced some communication glitches this month but they start to sort themselves out from today, thank goodness. Even so, you may have to help things along, perhaps by talking about what's gone wrong. If you suspect that an official letter has gone astray, you should take the initiative and find out what's happened to it.

• *Tuesday 21 December* •

If you're a typical Taurean you value both your emotional and physical security, and often tend to restrict your actions accordingly. But during the coming month you'll want to spread your wings more widely than usual, whether you do this through mental or physical pursuits. It will do you good to be more adventurous for a change, and to embrace life in all its aspects.

• *Wednesday 22 December* •

Time is hurtling towards Christmas Day and it seems that you're in a panic about how you're going to get everything done in time. You may even have reached the stage where you've ground to a halt because you don't know what to do first. So take a deep breath, calm down, and do things one at a time. Otherwise you'll end up feeling confused, tired and tearful.

• *Thursday 23 December* •

Someone isn't mucking about today, and if they're annoyed about something they'll come right out with it. This means you could be on the receiving end of some zingers, but equally it means that you'll be giving as good as you get. Now, although it will be very tempting to let off steam by giving someone an earful, aren't there better directions in which to channel your energy?

• *Friday 24 December* •

Keep calm! Your emotions are becoming increasingly heightened and intense today. As a result, you're likely to take things much more seriously than usual. That's wonderful if you're involved in a hot and heavy encounter with Mr or Ms Right, but it won't be such good news if you go overboard about silly trifles. If you're doing some last-minute shopping you'll want to be as extravagant as your budget allows. Or is it a case of 'Budget? What budget?'

• Saturday 25 December •

Happy Christmas! It looks like being a cracker of a day, with everyone doing their best to be great company. You're at your electrifying best, which is saying something, and your presence will definitely add to any gathering you attend. You might even manage to fit in some light-hearted flirting if you're really lucky. It's going to be a Christmas to remember.

• Sunday 26 December •

It's important that you leave yourself plenty of room for manoeuvre during the coming fortnight, especially when it comes to making decisions and airing your opinions. You need to be as flexible as possible right now; otherwise you could find that you've boxed yourself into a corner and have to do some serious backtracking. You need to consider all points of view and not just your own.

• Monday 27 December •

Make a big effort to spend time with people you didn't see on Christmas Day, especially if they're older than you or are having a bad time at the moment. You're brimming over with compassion and empathy, which will be really appreciated by anyone who's on the receiving end of your concern. You're also in the mood to make allowances for people, and that will help enormously.

• *Tuesday 28 December* •

If you've been neglecting that special someone in your life over the past few days because you've been so busy with the festivities, try to make up for it today. Maybe you could have some time alone with them, or perhaps you simply need to remind them how much you love them. Don't be afraid to open up your heart to them, and to let them do the same to you.

• *Wednesday 29 December* •

Someone gets in a bit of a muddle today and it could take some unravelling. For instance, they might get their wires crossed, leading to all sorts of misunderstandings. You might also encounter someone who is trying to rewrite history, perhaps because they can't bear to remember things as they really were. Should you set them straight or leave well alone?

• *Thursday 30 December* •

It's no good – the prospect of visiting the post-Christmas sales has become too inviting for you to resist any longer. No matter what you're doing today, you'll try to squeeze in the opportunity to dash around some of your favourite shops and see what's on offer. You could snap up some bargains but you should guard against the urge to splurge on items that you don't really want or need. The price of something may have been slashed but the acid test is whether you'd still buy it if it were full price. If not, leave it in the shop!

• *Friday 31 December* •

Friends and partners aren't behaving as you would like today. They're eager to go their own way, much to your annoyance.

In order to get round this you're going to have to ask yourself some tricky questions, such as whether you're trying to control everyone's behaviour or whether they're being inconsiderate in wanting to do their own thing. Maybe you should all release the tension by making it a super New Year's Eve celebration?

YOUR TAURUS SUN SIGN

In this chapter I am going to tell you all about your Taurus Sun sign. But what is a Sun sign? It often gets called a star sign, but are they the same thing? Well, yes, although 'Sun sign' is a more accurate term. Your Sun sign is the sign that the Sun occupied when you were born. Every year, the Sun moves through the heavens and spends an average of 30 days in each of the twelve signs. When you were born, the Sun was moving through the sign of Taurus, so this is your Sun or star sign.

This chapter tells you everything you want to know about your Sun sign. To start off, I describe your general personality – what makes you tick. Then I talk about your attitude to relationships, the way you handle money, what your Sun sign says about your health and, finally, which careers are best for you. Put all that together and you will have a well-rounded picture of yourself.

 Character

Everyone always knows where they stand with a Taurean. There is something very reliable, steadfast and reassuring about you, which comes as a great comfort to the rest of us. Anyone looking for the sort of person who will set the world on fire should forget about a Taurean, but if they want someone who honours their promises and who will be there through thick and thin, a Taurean should be top of their list.

As the sign of the bull, Taureans have a normally placid and easy-going nature and will tolerate all sorts of hassles without losing their temper. However, as anyone who's been chased by a rampaging bull knows, it's a different story when you become upset. If someone pushes you too far, they'll be on the receiving end of a massive row that they won't forget in a hurry.

Once you've reached a decision about something, it will take an earthquake to make you change your mind. Other people can go blue in the face trying to talk you round and you still won't agree with them. You see this as an example of your determination to stick to your guns. Anyone on the receiving end probably sees it as sheer stubbornness and obstinacy!

Change is another area in which you're reluctant to get involved. You have a very conservative streak and you certainly don't believe in changing things just for the sake of it. You believe that if it ain't broke, don't fix it. Even if it is broken, it might be better that way. However, there is a danger that this reluctance to initiate change can lead to a stick-in-the-mud tendency that prevails even when it works against your best interests.

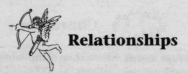 **Relationships**

Let's get one thing clear straight away: you belong to one of the two most attractive signs in the zodiac, an accolade you share with Librans. This means most Taureans are never short of admirers and probably even have to beat them off with a stick every now and then. Combine this with your natural modesty, charm and shyness, and it's an irresistible combination.

Yet most Taureans aren't interested in playing the field and breaking hearts left, right and centre. You're far too faithful and loyal for that. You're happiest if you can pair up with someone at an early age and stick to them like glue for the rest of your life. Infidelity is a massive no-no for you. You'd rather be accused of cheating at cards than of being unfaithful.

Emotional security is so important to you that occasionally you may try to help it along by keeping a watchful eye on your partner, just in case they might be doing something that will make you feel threatened. Unfortunately, this can sometimes spill over into possessiveness or jealousy, both of which can cause severe problems for many Taureans and their loved ones.

You have tremendous powers of affection and are very demonstrative. If you love someone, you want to show it. This means that sex is a vital part of life for you and you need a partner who shares your enthusiasm for it.

Money

Material security is essential to your happiness. You will endure all sorts of hardships with stoicism but one thing you want from a very early age is to own the roof over your head. You also need to know that you've got enough money coming in each week to feed yourself and your family. Food means a lot to you!

Taurus is a sign that understands and respects money, so you'll rarely fritter it away. However, that doesn't mean you don't enjoy spending it, because you do! It gives you great pleasure to buy objects that are beautiful or life-enhancing in some way. You are probably a canny investor, even though you may be reluctant to get involved in any high-risk investments. You'll certainly want to salt away as much spare cash as possible – it gives you a deliciously warm feeling to know you've got some funds to draw on when necessary. When you do have money to spare and you're looking for a good investment, you may well decide to put your money into bricks and mortar.

You're very careful to monitor your bank account and credit cards, to make sure everything is running smoothly. Some signs never look at their bank statements but you probably go through yours very carefully, making sure they don't contain any mistakes.

 **Health**

Taureans are usually happiest when they're in or near the countryside. It's partly because you're an Earth sign and partly because you're ruled by Venus, the planet of beauty. Put the two together and you're in clover – perhaps literally! A Taurean who lives in a high-rise flat miles from the nearest blade of grass will soon feel as though they've been cut off from their roots. They need a window box to look after or plenty of house plants in order to fulfil their Taurean love of nature.

It's vital for you to get plenty of fresh air, especially when life is tough. It's an important way for you to ground yourself and get everything in perspective once more. Ideally, you should do some gardening, even if that only means weeding your window box. It will soon bring a smile to your face.

The throat is the part of the body ruled by Taurus and you may find that this is your weak spot, especially when you're under a lot of pressure. You may be prone to lots of sore throats and may even lose your voice sometimes.

Your love of the good life can play havoc with your weight and many Taureans have to fight the battle of the bulge. If you can't give up your favourite comfort foods, you'll have to counteract them with plenty of exercise!

 **Career**

Taurus is the first of the Earth signs, which means exactly what it suggests – Taureans are very down to earth and sensible. You like to take life at a measured and steady pace, and are slightly suspicious of anyone who has a meteoric rise to the top. You believe you should work hard to achieve success and aren't comfortable with the idea of being given an easy ride.

You will certainly put a lot of effort into whatever you do for a living. Colleagues and superiors will appreciate your patience, perseverance and practicality. You are rarely flustered in a crisis and other people know they can depend on you. Sometimes, however, you may err on the side of caution and will be reluctant to make radical changes or get involved in anything that you think has more to do with fashion than sense. You can dig your heels in and refuse to budge!

Jobs that fit you like a glove are anything connected with the beauty or fashion businesses, horticulture, agriculture, floristry, finance and property. You may also enjoy working in a government department, especially if you think you can work your way to the top.

LOVE AND THE STARS

Have you ever noticed that you get on better with some signs than others? Perhaps all your friends belong to only a few signs or you've never hit it off with people who come from a particular sign. Or maybe you've recently met someone from a sign that you aren't familiar with at all, and you're wondering how your relationship will develop. Well, this chapter gives you a brief insight into your relationship with the other Sun signs. Check the combination under your own sign's heading first, then read about your relationship from the viewpoint of the other sign to find out what they think of you. It could be very revealing!

At the end of this chapter you'll find two compatibility charts that tell you, at a glance, how well you get on with the other signs as lovers and as friends. Look for the woman's Sun sign along the top of the chart and then find the man's sign down the side. The box where the two meet will show how well they get on together.

Even if your current relationship gets a low score from the charts, that doesn't mean it won't last. It simply indicates that you'll have to work harder at this relationship than at others.

Taurus

Taurus and **Taurus** is great because you're with someone who understands you inside out. Yet although this is comforting at first, it might start to become rather boring after a while, especially if you both like playing it safe.

Taurus and **Gemini** is good for keeping you on your toes, although you may find this tiring in the long term. They need a lot of change and variety, which can unsettle you and make you cling to stability and tradition.

Taurus and **Cancer** is lovely. You both appreciate the same sorts of things in life, such as good food, a loving partner and a cosy home. Once you get together you'll feel as though you've found your true soulmate.

Taurus and **Leo** share a love of luxury and the good things in life. You also know you can trust your Leo to be faithful and loyal, and in return you will shower them with plenty of admiration and moral support.

Taurus and **Virgo** is a very practical combination. Neither of you likes wasting time or money, although you may sometimes wish that your Virgo could be a little less austere and a bit more relaxed. But you still love them.

Taurus and **Libra** can have a very sensual and loving relationship. Neither of you likes conflict and you both need affectionate partners. But you may end up spending a lot of money together on all sorts of luxuries.

Taurus and **Scorpio** is a very powerful combination, especially in the bedroom. You both place a lot of importance on fidelity and loyalty, and you'll both believe that your relationship is the most important thing in your lives.

Taurus and **Sagittarius** don't really understand each other. You enjoy your home comforts and are generally content with life, while your Sagittarian always finds the grass is greener on the other side of the fence.

Taurus and **Capricorn** have a lot in common. You're both lusty, earthy and full of common sense. If you aren't careful, your relationship could get bogged down in practicalities, making you neglect the fun side of things.

Taurus and **Aquarius** struggle to appreciate each other. You enjoy sticking to the status quo whenever possible, while your Aquarian is always thinking of the future. You're both very stubborn, so rows can end in stalemate.

Taurus and **Pisces** is fine if your Piscean has their feet on the ground, because then you'll enjoy their sensitivity. But if they're very vague or other-worldly, you'll soon get annoyed and lose patience with them.

Taurus and **Aries** isn't the easiest combination for you. Although you enjoy your Arien's enthusiasm, it can wear a bit thin sometimes, especially when they're keen on something that you think is unrealistic or too costly.

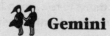 **Gemini**

Gemini and **Gemini** can be great fun or one big headache. You both crave variety and busy lives, but if you're both very sociable you may rarely see each other. Your sex life may also fizzle out over time.

Gemini and **Cancer** is tricky if you're lovers rather than friends. Although you'll adore your Cancerian's displays of affection at first, after a while they may seem rather clingy or will make you feel trapped.

Gemini and **Leo** have lots of fun together. You genuinely like and love one another, although you may secretly be amused sometimes by your Leo's regal behaviour and want to give them some gentle teasing.

Gemini and **Virgo** hit it off surprisingly well. There's so much for you to talk about and plenty of scope for having a good laugh. You're tremendous friends, whether your relationship is sexual or purely platonic.

Gemini and **Libra** is one of the most enjoyable combinations of all for you. You can encourage your easy-going Libran to be more assertive while they help you to relax, and also bring out the romance in your soul.

Gemini and **Scorpio** make uncomfortable bedfellows but good friends. You have very little in common sexually but are intrigued by each other's minds. You share an insatiable curiosity about human nature.

Gemini and **Sagittarius** have a really good time together. You especially enjoy learning new things from one another and never run out of things to talk about. Travel and books are just two of your many shared enthusiasms.

Gemini and **Capricorn** isn't very easy because you're so different. At first you're intrigued by your Capricorn's responsibility and common sense, but after a while they may seem a little staid or stuffy for you.

Gemini and **Aquarius** are fantastic friends. You're used to having the upper hand intellectually with people but here is someone who makes you think and encourages you to look at life in a new way.

Gemini and **Pisces** can be tricky because it's easy to hurt your Piscean's feelings without even realizing it. Neither of you is very keen on facing up to harsh reality, which causes problems if you both avoid dealing with the facts.

Gemini and **Aries** is tremendous fun and you'll spend a lot of time laughing. If even half the plans you make come to fruition, you'll have a fantastic time together with never a dull moment.

Gemini and **Taurus** can make you wonder what you're doing wrong. Your Taurean may seem bemused or even slightly alarmed by you, and positively threatened by your need for as much variety in your life as possible.

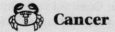 **Cancer**

Cancer and **Cancer** is wonderful because you're able to take refuge in each other. You'll lavish a lot of time and effort on your home. Problems will arise if one of you doesn't get on well with the other one's family or friends.

Cancer and **Leo** share a love of family life, and you may even agree to give it priority over everything else. You'll be very proud of your Leo's achievements but will fret if these take them away from home too often.

Cancer and **Virgo** have a lot to teach each other. You'll learn from your Virgo how to do things methodically and carefully, and you'll encourage them to be more demonstrative and loving. It should work well!

Cancer and **Libra** is great if you have shared goals. You both understand the importance of ambition and will readily support one another. You enjoy being with someone who isn't afraid to show their affection.

Cancer and **Scorpio** is a very emotional and satisfying pairing. You know you can reveal your true feelings to your Scorpio, and you'll encourage them to do the same with you. Sexually, you'll really be in your element.

Cancer and **Sagittarius** find it hard to appreciate each other. You may even feel as though you come from different planets because you operate on a very emotional level while your Sagittarian prefers to stick to the facts.

Cancer and **Capricorn** is a case of opposites attracting. You both need what the other one can offer, and you'll be especially pleased if your Capricorn's capacity for hard work will provide a roof over your head and a stable home.

Cancer and **Aquarius** can be quirky friends but you'll struggle to sustain an emotional relationship because you're chalk and cheese. Your need for love and reassurance may be very difficult for your Aquarian to deal with.

Cancer and **Pisces** are really happy together. It's great knowing that you're with someone who understands your deep emotional needs and your complicated personality. You'll also revel in taking care of your Piscean.

Cancer and **Aries** can work if you both make allowances for each other. You need to give your Aries a lot of freedom because they'll get very angry if they feel they're tied to your apron strings.

Cancer and **Taurus** is a marriage made in heaven. You both need a happy, comfortable home and you also share a love of food. Your relationship may be so self-sufficient that you barely need anyone else in your lives.

Cancer and **Gemini** is OK if you don't spend too much time together! You'll feel slightly threatened by your Gemini's need for an active and independent social life, and they'll resent being expected to spend so much time at home.

 Leo

Leo and **Leo** is a very strong combination but there could be a few battles for power every now and then. After all, neither of you likes to relinquish the reins and hand over control to anyone else. Even so, you'll have a lot of fun.

Leo and **Virgo** is fine if you're prepared for some give and take but it won't be very easy if each of you stands your ground. You'll be pleased if your Virgo tries to help or advise you, but will be hurt if this turns to undue criticism.

Leo and **Libra** is a delicious pairing because it brings together the two signs of love. You'll adore being with someone who is so considerate, although their lack of decisiveness may sometimes make you grit your teeth with irritation.

Leo and **Scorpio** is wonderful until you have a row. At that point, you'll both refuse to budge an inch and admit that you might be in the wrong. You both set a lot of store by status symbols, which could work out expensive.

Leo and **Sagittarius** is great for keeping each other amused. You're both enthusiastic, intuitive and expansive, although you could sometimes be annoyed if your Sagittarian's social life prevents you seeing much of them.

Leo and **Capricorn** share a tremendous love of family and you'll enjoy creating a happy home together. Don't expect your Capricorn to be instinctively demonstrative: you may have to teach them to be more open.

Leo and **Aquarius** understand each other even if you don't always see eye to eye. Sometimes you can be left speechless by your plain-speaking Aquarian, and disappointed by their occasional reluctance to be cuddly.

Leo and **Pisces** bring out each other's creativity. This is a superb artistic partnership but may not be such good news if you're trying to maintain a sexual relationship because you have so little in common.

Leo and **Aries** have terrific fun together and will share many adventures. You'll enjoy making lots of plans, even if they don't always work out. You'll also spend plenty of money on lavishly entertaining your friends.

Leo and **Taurus** is the sort of relationship that makes you feel you know where you stand. You love knowing that your

Taurean is steadfast and true, and that together you make a formidable team.

Leo and **Gemini** is a fun-filled combination that you really enjoy. You're stunned by your Gemini's endless inventiveness and their versatility, although you may secretly believe that they spread themselves too thin.

Leo and **Cancer** is great if you both need a comfortable and cosy home. But you may soon feel hemmed in if your Cancerian wants to restrict your social circle to nothing but family and close friends. You need more scope than that.

 **Virgo**

Virgo and **Virgo** can endure many storms together, even though it's tough going at times. Here is someone who completely understands your interesting mixture of quirky individualism and the need to conform.

Virgo and **Libra** get on well together up to a point but can then come unstuck. It annoys you when your Libran fails to stand up for themselves and you don't understand why they're so touchy when you point out their faults.

Virgo and **Scorpio** are both fascinated by the details of life and you'll spend many happy hours analysing people's characters. Try not to be too brusque when pointing out some of your Scorpio's stranger points; they won't like it!

Virgo and **Sagittarius** is a very sociable pairing and you'll enjoy being together. You'll also have some fascinating conversations in which you both learn a lot. Sexually, it will either be great or ghastly.

Virgo and **Capricorn** really understand each other. You appreciate your Capricorn's reliability but worry about their workaholic tendencies. You'll both benefit from being openly affectionate and loving with one another.

Virgo and **Aquarius** enjoy discussing just about everything under the sun. But you'll quickly get irritated by your Aquarian's idiosyncratic views and their insistence that they're always right. Surely if anyone's right, you are?

Virgo and **Pisces** is not the easiest combination you can choose. If your Piscean finds it hard to face up to reality, you won't be sympathetic because you simply can't understand such an ostrich-like attitude.

Virgo and **Aries** struggle to get on well as close partners. You simply don't understand each other. They make a mess and you like things to be tidy. They rush into things and you like to take your time. There is little common ground.

Virgo and **Taurus** love each other's company. You both like to keep your feet on the ground and you share a healthy respect for money. You also have a very raunchy time in the bedroom although you don't advertise that fact.

Virgo and **Gemini** is a super combination for friendship or business. You think along similar lines and both excel at being flexible. However, in a sexual relationship you may fail to appreciate each other's finer points.

Virgo and **Cancer** is a great team. You like to take care of worldly matters while your Cancerian creates a happy and cosy home. If they collect a lot of clutter you'll think of it as dust traps rather than delightful keepsakes.

Virgo and **Leo** find it hard to understand each other because you're so different. You may secretly find your Leo rather ostentatious and there could be rows about the amount of money they spend. Try to live and let live.

 Libra

Libra and **Libra** get on really well provided at least one of you is decisive and able to say what they think sometimes. You'll appreciate one another's consideration, sensitivity and intelligence. A great combination!

Libra and **Scorpio** are good friends but may not understand each other's sexual and emotional needs. You may feel uncomfortable with the brooding, intense moods of your Scorpio, wishing they took things less seriously.

Libra and **Sagittarius** have lots of fun together, especially when it comes to discussing ideas and taking off on jaunts. However, you could be rather nonplussed, and possibly even hurt, by your Sagittarian's blunt comments.

Libra and **Capricorn** get on famously if you share goals. You understand each other's need to work hard towards your ambitions. But you'll have to coax your Capricorn into being as demonstrative and loving as you'd like.

Libra and **Aquarius** appreciate one another's minds. You may be better friends than lovers, because you could be bemused and hurt if your Aquarian is unnerved by your need for romance and idealism.

Libra and **Pisces** share a need for peace and harmony. You'll adore being with someone who's so artistic and sensitive, but you both need to balance your romantic natures with hefty doses of reality every now and then.

Libra and **Aries** are a great example of how opposites can attract. You admire the way your brave Arien can be so outspoken, and they may even manage to teach you to stand up for yourself.

Libra and **Taurus** share a love of beauty and an appreciation of the finer things in life. At first you may think you've found your perfect partner, although you may get irritated if your Taurean is very placid.

Libra and **Gemini** get on well in every sort of relationship. You're amused by your Gemini's butterfly ability to flit from one topic to the next and will enjoy encouraging them to discover the romance that lurks inside them.

Libra and **Cancer** enjoy one another's company. You love the way your Cancerian so obviously cares about your welfare and happiness, and it does you good to be the one who's fussed over for a change.

Libra and **Leo** can be a very expensive combination! Neither of you is frightened to spend money and together you can have a field day. Emotionally, you revel in one another's company because you're both born romantics.

Libra and **Virgo** have to make a lot of effort to appreciate one another. You can understand the importance of attending to details but you may secretly think that your Virgo sometimes is too much of a nit-picker.

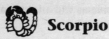 **Scorpio**

Scorpio and **Scorpio** feel safe with each other. You both know what you're capable of, good and bad. It's great to be with someone who matches you for intensity, but you might wind each other up and feed each other's neuroses.

Scorpio and **Sagittarius** can miss each other by miles. Even as friends, it's hard to understand one another. You like to zero in on the details while your Sagittarian prefers to take a broad view of the entire situation.

Scorpio and **Capricorn** bring out the best in one another, but it can take a little time. You enjoy the serious side to your Capricorn but you can also have some great laughs together. You also love knowing that they're so reliable.

Scorpio and **Aquarius** can have some terrific rows! You both have a tendency to be dogmatic and it's even worse when you get together. You can feel threatened if your Aquarian isn't as openly affectionate as you'd like.

Scorpio and **Pisces** share some powerful moments together. You love the complexity and sensitivity of your Piscean but will soon become suspicious if you think they're holding out on you or are playing games behind your back.

Scorpio and **Aries** is a tempestuous combination. Your temper builds up from a slow burn while your Arien will have a quick tantrum and then forget about it. Sexually, you'll have more than met your match.

Scorpio and **Taurus** complement each other in many ways. You're both loyal and loving, and you both need a secure home. However, problems will arise if one or both of you is possessive and jealous.

Scorpio and **Gemini** hit it off as friends but will struggle to stick together as lovers. You like to explore the nitty-gritty of situations while your Gemini apparently prefers to skim the surface. You may wonder if you can trust them.

Scorpio and **Cancer** can enjoy a highly emotional and satisfying relationship. You understand one another's needs and will take great delight in creating a stable and happy home life together.

Scorpio and **Leo** is tricky if you both want to rule the roost. Neither of you likes to relinquish control of situations, which can lead to some stormy battles for power. At times you may be jealous of your Leo's huge circle of friends.

Scorpio and **Virgo** have some wonderfully analytical conversations. You both enjoy digging below the surface to find out what's really going on. If it's a sexual relationship, its success will rest on what happens in the bedroom.

Scorpio and **Libra** appreciate one another but you may sometimes wish your Libran could be more forceful and dynamic. It will drive you mad when they sit on the fence or bend over backwards to please everyone.

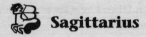 **Sagittarius**

Sagittarius and **Sagittarius** will either have a whale of a time or never see each other. If you both have wide-ranging interests, it may be difficult to make enough time for one another and you may eventually drift apart.

Sagittarius and **Capricorn** think of each other as a creature from another planet. You like your Capricorn's common sense but will soon get fed up if they cling to tradition, are a workaholic or never want to take any risks.

Sagittarius and **Aquarius** have a fantastic time together. You share so many interests that there is always something to talk about, with some far-ranging discussions. But you may wish your Aquarian were less pedantic.

Sagittarius and **Pisces** enjoy being friends but it can be difficult to understand each other as lovers. You like your Piscean's sensitivity but wish they weren't quite so easily hurt when you make off-the-cuff comments.

Sagittarius and **Aries** is great fun. You'll have all sorts of adventures together, with exotic holidays a particular indulgence. You're both pretty outspoken and your no-holds-barred rows will raise the roof.

Sagittarius and **Taurus** struggle to hit it off. You're so different that it's hard to find much common ground. If your Taurean is possessive, you'll soon feel trapped and want to break free, or decide to do things behind their back.

Sagittarius and **Gemini** is a super combination. You have masses in common and are endlessly intrigued by one another. However, you must be friends as well as lovers, otherwise you may soon get bored with each other.

Sagittarius and **Cancer** can't make each other out at all. You're mystified by your Cancerian's constant need for their home and family, and will be irritated if you think they're too parochial and unadventurous.

Sagittarius and **Leo** revel in each other's company, especially when it comes to having fun. This can be an expensive pairing because you both enjoy living it up whenever you get the chance. Shopping trips will also be costly.

Sagittarius and **Virgo** is OK up to a point. You enjoy each other's brains but you'll soon lose patience if your Virgo is very finicky and anxious. You like to let your hair down but they may always worry about the consequences.

Sagittarius and **Libra** like each other, whether as friends, family or lovers. You have enough similarities to find some common ground but enough differences to keep things interesting. It's an intriguing combination.

Sagittarius and **Scorpio** try and fail to understand each other. You like to take life as it comes and can't stand your Scorpio's tendency to plot things in advance. You'll hate it if they're suspicious or jealous of you.

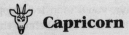 **Capricorn**

Capricorn and **Capricorn** feel very safe together. At last you're with someone who understands you, and who's as reliable and responsible as you. However, this may mean that your work clashes with your relationship.

Capricorn and **Aquarius** is either a big hit or a big no-no. You both need to compromise and be willing to learn from each other for it to work. Your love of convention will be sorely challenged by your radical Aquarian.

Capricorn and **Pisces** can learn a lot from each other as friends. You'll learn to be more sensitive and open-minded. However, you'll soon be turned off if your Piscean is reluctant to face up to facts and be realistic.

Capricorn and **Aries** support each other in many ways. You're both ambitious and will respect one another's goals. You'll enjoy teaching your Arien to be more responsible, and they'll teach you how to play.

Capricorn and **Taurus** feel safe with one another. You both understand the importance of tradition and share the need to do things properly. You can get surprisingly earthy and intense in the bedroom.

Capricorn and **Gemini** don't really hit it off. You're amused by your Gemini but you may secretly think they're too flighty and superficial for you. It's difficult to find much common ground sexually or emotionally.

Capricorn and **Cancer** really enjoy each other's company. You both adore having someone to take care of, and if anyone can dissuade you from working round the clock it's a home-cooking, sensuous and affectionate Cancerian.

Capricorn and **Leo** both like the best in life but you won't be as willing to pay for it as your Leo. In fact, you may be seriously worried by their extravagance and also slightly wearied by their demanding social life.

Capricorn and **Virgo** go together like bread and butter. However, there may not be much jam if you're both careful with your money. If you share a home you'll want it to be traditional, with conventional family values.

Capricorn and **Libra** have a healthy respect for each other. You love your Libran's diplomacy and tact, because you know you can take them anywhere and they'll fit in. They'll also encourage you to open up emotionally.

Capricorn and **Scorpio** is a very businesslike pairing. You excel at making money together, no matter what your relationship. Sometimes you can be put off by the intense and complex passions of your Scorpio.

Capricorn and **Sagittarius** can be strange. You like each other for your curiosity value if not much else. Even so, your Sagittarian will teach you to be more broad-minded and relaxed, if you let them.

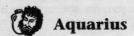 **Aquarius**

Aquarius and **Aquarius** is either wonderful or too much like hard work. One if not both of you must be willing to compromise sometimes, otherwise it will be continual stalemate. You'll have formidable battles of intellect.

Aquarius and **Pisces** is tricky. You don't understand each other, and the more unworldly and unrealistic your Piscean, the more dogmatic and precise you'll become in retaliation. You can easily hurt each other.

Aquarius and **Aries** are great sparring partners and you'll love every minute of it. Your Arien isn't afraid to stand up to you and to fight their corner. They'll also teach you a thing or two about sexual relationships.

Aquarius and **Taurus** is fine all the while you agree with each other. But, at the first hint of dissent, it will be war. Your need for emotional and intellectual freedom will clash with your Taurean's need for closeness.

Aquarius and **Gemini** are firm friends. You enjoy intense intellectual discussions and your Gemini will teach you to be more free-thinking and flexible. Try not to analyse your relationship out of existence.

Aquarius and **Cancer** can be an uneasy combination. You have little in common and don't understand each other. At first you'll enjoy being taken care of by your Cancerian but you may soon feel suffocated and trapped.

Aquarius and **Leo** enjoy each other's company. You love your Leo's exuberance and marvel at their social skills. You'll also be very impressed by their ability to organize you and make your life run so smoothly.

Aquarius and **Virgo** can seem like hard work. It's easier to be friends than lovers because you have such different views of the world. You enjoy pitting your wits against each other in wide-ranging discussions.

Aquarius and **Libra** is great fun and you love sharing ideas. If you get involved in an emotional relationship, your Libran will encourage you to be more demonstrative and less analytical about your feelings.

Aquarius and **Scorpio** is a very powerful combination because you're both so sure of yourselves. In the inevitable disputes, neither of you will want to back down. You may also be turned off by your Scorpio's complicated emotions.

Aquarius and **Sagittarius** enjoy each other's company. You also share a love of learning and both need as much intellectual freedom as you can get. This can be a very enduring relationship, whether it's platonic or passionate.

Aquarius and **Capricorn** will give you lots to think about because you'll be so busy trying to work out what makes each other tick. You may never arrive at an answer! You need to find some middle ground and to compromise.

 **Pisces**

Pisces and **Pisces** is wonderful if you're both prepared to face facts rather than pretend your relationship is something it's not. Your life is likely to be highly romantic and you'll love creating a sophisticated home together.

Pisces and **Aries** will be very trying at times. It may also be painful, since your Arien is unlikely to understand how easily you're hurt. Even so, they will encourage you to grow another layer of skin and to laugh at yourself.

Pisces and **Taurus** is a very sensual combination. You'll bring out the romantic in one another, but there will be times when you'll wish your Taurean were less matter-of-fact, practical and sensible.

Pisces and **Gemini** can have fun together but it's awfully easy for you to feel hurt by your Gemini's glib turns of phrase.

You may be happier as friends than lovers because your emotional needs are so different.

Pisces and **Cancer** is super because you both express love in the same way. It's wonderful being with someone who takes such care of you, although your Cancerian may not understand your need to be left alone sometimes.

Pisces and **Leo** find it hard to understand each other. At times you may find your Leo rather grand. You share a pronounced artistic streak and you're both very affectionate, but is that enough to keep you together?

Pisces and **Virgo** can be difficult for you. Your Virgo may trample all over your feelings in their well-meaning efforts to point out your faults and help you to rise above them. It all sounds like a lot of unnecessary criticism to you.

Pisces and **Libra** can be incredibly romantic. You could easily have a heady affair straight out of a Hollywood weepie, but staying together is another matter. You may drift apart because you're reluctant to face up to problems.

Pisces and **Scorpio** is a highly emotional and complex pairing. You're both very deep and sensitive, and it may take a while before you begin to understand each other. Once that happens, you won't look back.

Pisces and **Sagittarius** is dicey because you won't know what to make of your forthright Sagittarian. Why are they so blunt? Can't they see that it upsets you? You may be better as friends who share lots of exploits.

Pisces and **Capricorn** is fine if your Capricorn is happy to show their feelings. But if they're buttoned up or repressed, you won't know how to get through to them. Even so, you'll love the way they provide for you.

Pisces and **Aquarius** may as well be talking different languages for all the sense you make to each other. They enjoy talking about ideas that leave you baffled but will struggle to express their emotions in the way you need.

 Aries

Aries and **Aries** is a very energetic combination, and you encourage each other in many different ways. Your relationship is competitive, sexy, exciting and sometimes pretty tempestuous!

Aries and **Taurus** can be difficult because you don't always understand each other. You love your Taurean's loyalty and affection but can feel frustrated if they're a great traditionalist or very stubborn.

Aries and **Gemini** get on like a house on fire and love hatching up new schemes together. But your differing sexual needs could cause problems, especially if your Gemini doesn't share your high sex drive.

Aries and **Cancer** is fine if your Cancerian will give you lots of personal freedom. However, they may be hurt if you aren't at home as much as they'd like, and they'll wonder what you're up to while you're away.

Aries and **Leo** really hit it off well and you'll have a lot of fun together. Sometimes you may wish your Leo would unbend a bit and be less dignified, but you adore the way they love and cherish you. It's great for your ego!

Aries and **Virgo** can be tricky because you have so little in common. You like to rush through life taking each day as it comes while they prefer to plan things in advance and then worry if they're doing the right thing. Irritating!

Aries and **Libra** have a lot to learn from each other. You enjoy the odd skirmish while your Libran prefers to keep the peace. Try to compromise over your differences rather than make them either/or situations.

Aries and **Scorpio** can be very dynamic and sexy together. Power is a huge aphrodisiac for you both so you're greatly attracted to each other. If you're a flirtatious Aries, your Scorpio will soon clip your wings.

Aries and **Sagittarius** are really excited by each other's company. You both adore challenges and will spur one another on to further feats and adventures. Your sex life is lively and interesting, and will keep you pretty busy.

Aries and **Capricorn** may not seem to have much in common on the surface. Yet you are both ambitious and will enjoy watching each other's progress. Sexually, things are surprisingly highly charged and naughty.

Aries and **Aquarius** have a lot of fun together but also share plenty of sparring matches. You get on better as friends than lovers because your Aquarian may not be nearly as interested in sex as you are.

Aries and **Pisces** is one of those tricky combinations that needs a lot of care if it's to succeed. It's horribly easy for you to upset your Piscean, often without realizing it, and you may get bored with having to reassure them so much.

Compatibility in Love and Sex at a glance

F M	♈	♉	♊	♋	♌	♍	♎	♏	♐	♑	♒	♓
♈	8	5	9	7	9	4	7	8	9	7	7	3
♉	6	8	4	10	7	8	8	7	3	8	2	8
♊	8	2	7	3	8	7	9	4	9	4	9	4
♋	5	10	4	8	6	5	6	8	2	9	2	8
♌	9	8	9	7	7	4	9	6	8	7	9	6
♍	4	8	6	4	4	7	6	7	7	9	4	4
♎	7	8	10	7	8	5	9	6	9	6	10	6
♏	7	9	4	7	6	6	7	10	5	6	5	7
♐	9	4	10	4	9	7	8	4	9	6	9	5
♑	7	8	4	9	6	8	6	4	4	8	4	5
♒	8	6	9	4	9	4	9	6	8	7	8	2
♓	7	6	7	9	6	7	6	9	7	5	4	9

1 = the pits
10 = the peaks

Key

♈ – Aries
♉ – Taurus
♊ – Gemini
♋ – Cancer
♌ – Leo
♍ – Virgo

♎ – Libra
♏ – Scorpio
♐ – Sagittarius
♑ – Capricorn
♒ – Aquarius
♓ – Pisces

Compatibility in Friendship at a glance

M \ F	♈	♉	♊	♋	♌	♍	♎	♏	♐	♑	♒	♓
♈	8	5	10	5	9	3	7	8	9	6	8	5
♉	6	9	6	10	7	8	7	6	4	9	3	9
♊	9	3	9	4	9	8	10	5	10	5	10	6
♋	6	9	4	9	5	4	6	9	4	10	3	9
♌	10	7	9	6	9	4	8	6	9	6	9	7
♍	5	9	8	4	4	8	5	8	8	10	5	6
♎	8	9	10	8	8	6	9	5	9	6	10	7
♏	7	8	5	8	7	7	6	9	4	5	6	8
♐	9	5	10	4	10	8	8	4	10	7	9	6
♑	6	9	5	10	6	9	5	5	4	9	5	6
♒	9	6	10	5	9	5	9	7	9	5	9	3
♓	6	7	6	10	6	8	7	9	8	6	4	10

1 = the pits
10 = the peaks

Key

♈ – Aries	♎ – Libra
♉ – Taurus	♏ – Scorpio
♊ – Gemini	♐ – Sagittarius
♋ – Cancer	♑ – Capricorn
♌ – Leo	♒ – Aquarius
♍ – Virgo	♓ – Pisces

YOUR ASTROLOGICAL HOLIDAY GUIDE

Have you ever wondered which holiday destination is right for your Sun sign, and what sort of activities you'll most enjoy when you get there? Well, your questions have been answered because this guide will give you some great ideas about how to have the holiday of a lifetime.

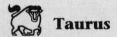 **Taurus**

As the great hedonist of the zodiac, your idea of a blissful holiday is one in which you do as little as possible while other people attend to your every whim. If money is no object you'll be in seventh heaven staying in a luxury hotel that serves delectable drinks, sumptuous food and has the finest cotton sheets. Some signs are completely incapable of sitting around doing nothing but you could turn it into an art form, given half a chance. If you have to lower your holiday sights through a lack of cash, you'd enjoy staying in a self-catering cottage in beautiful surroundings. The cottage must have all mod cons, of course, because the charm of pumping your own water from a tumbledown well would pall after the first ten minutes. You feel revived and rejuvenated when you're surrounded by nature and beauty, so you might enjoy a holiday tour of famous gardens, a visit to a country renowned for its autumn colours or a trip to an unspoilt island paradise.

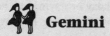

Gemini

Variety is the spice of life for you, so you won't want to visit the same destination year after year. Instead, you like the thought of trying somewhere completely different each time, because half the fun is reading about it before you go and then trying to cram a selection of indispensable travel guides and phrase books into your already bulging suitcase. You need to keep on the move, too, so are happiest if the local transport is excellent or you can hire a car to get around. You're thrilled by bustling cities, especially if you can sit in a café and watch the world go by, then shop to your heart's content. Destinations that are steeped in history or culture also appeal to you. Another option is to take an activity holiday in which you'll learn something new; it could be anything from watercolour painting to belly-dancing.

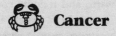

Cancer

Familiarity breeds content for you, so you can feel uneasy when visiting somewhere for the first time. What if you don't like it? You're the sort of person who is welcomed with open arms by hoteliers because if you like the place you'll return year after year, and you'll take your nearest and dearest with you. It's a rare Cancerian who doesn't enjoy eating, so you'll want to choose a destination in which the food is to your liking, and you'll hope that there's lots of it. You can't cope with anything too exotic or strange, and you need to take care of your sensitive tummy, which rules out some of the more far-flung corners of the world. You also can't tolerate extreme heat or humidity. You love being near water and would enjoy a relaxing beach holiday or staying at a hotel on a large lake. Another option is a self-catering holiday in which you can create a home from home.

 Leo

The one thing you crave above all else is sunshine, so it's very high up on your list of holiday priorities. You really come into your own when you're in a hot climate, although even you will wilt if the temperature rises too high. If you could have your heart's desire, you'd stay in a luxurious and exclusive resort on a tropical island, where you could do lots of celebrity-spotting while sipping cocktails on a palm-fringed beach. Too expensive? Then you would love going on safari and seeing your namesake lions prowling around, provided you didn't have to hammer in your own tent pegs every night. You do have your standards! Something else that would appeal is driving through a warm and friendly country in a chic or classic car, staying at delightful hotels along the way and buying lots of lovely clothes to wear when you get home.

Virgo

Although you may sound enthusiastic when your friends tell you about their trips to exotic locations, or describe meals containing the sort of wriggly items that you would squash to death if you found them in your garden, in reality you avoid them like the plague. Actually, you would probably rather have the plague than visit anywhere with dodgy hygiene, unsafe drinking water, poisonous creepy-crawlies, stomach-churning food or primitive plumbing. You're not the most adventurous traveller in the world and you don't care! Ideal holiday destinations for you include ski resorts where you can get exercise, hot chocolate and fresh air, or luxurious health farms that serve more than just a single lettuce leaf once a day. You would also adore a specialist holiday which caters for one of your interests and keeps your very clever brain fully occupied.

 Libra

You can take any amount of luxury, relaxation and lotus-eating, especially when you're on holiday. You're too intelligent to be content spending a fortnight lying on a beach, but you might fancy visiting somewhere that offers the twin attractions of sparkling blue seas and plenty of culture. Decent food will also be high on your list of holiday essentials, because there's nothing you like better than working your way through a menu full of delicious temptations. You may even choose your destination or hotel purely on the strength of its cuisine or wine, and you'll do your best to sample as much of it as possible. If you're a typical Libran you have very sophisticated tastes and would enjoy visiting one of the great cities of the world, especially if you can combine sightseeing with an enjoyable tour of the best shops you can find.

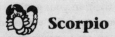

Scorpio

You take such an intense approach to life that regular breaks are essential for you, because they help you to get things back in perspective. What's more, you're prepared to spend quite a lot of money on a holiday if necessary. If you can only take a short break, you adore the thought of staying in a fabulous country hotel, complete with spa, swimming pool, gardens and Michelin-starred dining room. So what if the bill makes your eyes water? You'll have had more than your money's worth in terms of enjoyment. You soon get bored if nothing is going on, so an activity holiday is perfect for you, especially if it offers plenty of excitement. You could learn to scuba-dive, brush up your skiing, go potholing or practise body-surfing. If you fancy something less daredevil, you might consider a wine-tasting holiday, a murder-mystery weekend or an Antarctic cruise.

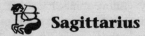

Sagittarius

If you're a dyed-in-the-wool Sagittarian, you've probably already chosen the destinations of your next ten holidays. Travel is in your blood and you love exploring the world. You're unlikely to want to revisit the same place twice, although you might develop an abiding passion for a particular country and enjoy visiting different parts of it over the years. In the end, you'll be quite an expert on the subject. Your ideal holiday offers a combination of delicious food and drink, breathtaking scenery, comfortable sleeping arrangements, plenty of history, loads of culture and lots to look at. Grilling on a beach for two weeks, looking only at the sand, is your idea of hell. You'd much rather jump on a local bus and see where it takes you, laze the afternoon away in a restaurant or put your guidebook through its paces. You enjoy both heat and cold, which means you can be happy almost anywhere in the world.

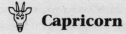

🐐 Capricorn

You aren't entirely convinced by the need for holidays because they can seem like such an extravagance to you. Deep down, you'd probably rather stay at home and feel good about the money you've saved. If you are persuaded to go away, you won't want to throw your cash around willy-nilly and will choose somewhere that doesn't cost the earth. Nevertheless, you aren't keen on places that are too cheap and cheerful, and you're quite choosy about the company you keep. You might enjoy a skiing holiday, rock climbing or simply relaxing high in the mountains somewhere. You're very practical, so would also appreciate a holiday in which you learn a new skill or craft. You have a strong conservative streak, so will avoid anywhere that's too exotic, strange or dangerous. Instead, you'll choose places that feel familiar, and preferably where there's no language barrier.

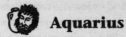 **Aquarius**

The last thing you want to do on holiday is be surrounded by crowds and feel that you're part of a gigantic marketing machine. Instead, you're drawn to places that are off the beaten track, unfashionable (so you don't have to rub shoulders with every Tom, Dick and Harry) or are yet to be discovered by most people. You have no interest in simple beach holidays, unless you can alternate sunbathing with plenty of sightseeing. Destinations steeped in history and culture are ideal for you, because you love tuning in to the atmosphere and learning more about the country you're visiting. It's also essential that the place offers peace and quiet, so you can read all those books you've brought with you. For you, part of the pleasure of going on holiday is meeting the locals, so it's important that you visit somewhere friendly and welcoming.

 **Pisces**

You're so sensitive to atmospheres that you need to choose your holiday destination very carefully. Try to avoid political trouble spots or places that are heaving with fellow holiday-makers because your delicate nerves will soon become jangled and you'll start longing to go home again. You adore being near water, whether it's a lake or an ocean, and find it very relaxing just to listen to the sound of the waves while gazing into space. The clear blue waters of a tropical island would be paradise for you, because you love swimming. You aren't comfortable if you have to rough it, so are happiest staying somewhere that offers plenty of luxury. However, you'll be very disturbed if there's a marked contrast between your level of comfort and that of the local people. Your ideal holiday includes plenty of sightseeing, because you love soaking up the atmosphere and getting a strong sense of the spirit of the place.

Aries

In an ideal world, you would never visit the same holiday destination twice because you hate that sense of 'been there, done that'. Besides, there's a whole world out there waiting to be explored, so why waste your valuable holiday time going back to the same old resort year after year? If you're a typical Arien, excitement, heat and plenty of action are the ingredients for a perfect holiday. If a little courage is required, then so much the better. You'll enjoy regaling your friends and family with eye-popping tales of your bravery as you mastered white-water rafting, braved huge rollers on your surfboard, went on safari, trekked through a jungle or endured the baking heat of a desert. If you have to choose something that you consider to be more tame, you'll enjoy a fly-drive or activity holiday. At a pinch, you might be persuaded to lie on a beach but you won't want to do it for long because you'll soon get bored.

BORN ON THE CUSP?

Were you born on the cusp of Taurus – at the beginning or end of the sign? If so, you may have spent years wondering which sign you belong to. Are you a Taurean, an Arien or a Gemini? Different horoscope books and columns can give different dates for when the Sun moves into each sign, leaving you utterly confused. Yet none of these dates is wrong, as you'll discover in a minute. Checking your birth date, and time if you know it, in the list given in this chapter will allow you to solve the mystery at long last!

Many people believe that the Sun moves like clockwork from one sign to another on a specific day each year. But this isn't always true. For instance, let's look at the dates for the sign of Taurus. On the cover of this book I give them as 21 April to 21 May. Very often, the Sun will obediently change signs on these days but sometimes it won't. It can move from Aries into Taurus on 19, 20 or 21 April and it can move into Gemini on 20, 21 or 22 May.

So how can you find out which sign you belong to if you were born on the cusp of Taurus? The only information you need is the place, year, day and the time of your birth if you know it. It helps to have the time of birth because if the Sun did move signs on your birthday, you can see whether it moved before or after you were born. If you don't have an exact time, even knowing whether it was morning or after-noon can be a help. For instance, if you were born in the morning and the Sun didn't move signs on your birthday until the afternoon, that will be enough information to tell you which sign is yours.

You need to know the place in case you were born outside the United Kingdom and have to convert its local time zone to British time. This information is easily available in many diaries and reference books.

Four Simple Steps to Find your Sun Sign

1 Write down the year, day, time and place of your birth, in that order.
2 If you were born outside the United Kingdom, you must convert your birth date and time to British time by adding or subtracting the relevant number of hours from your birth time to convert it to British time. This may take your birthday into the following day or back to the previous day. If so, write down this new date and time because that will be the one you use in the following calculations. If summer time was oper-ating you must deduct the relevant number of hours to convert your birth time to Greenwich Mean Time (GMT).
3 If you were born in Britain, look up your year of birth in the list of British Summer Time (BST) changes to see if BST was operating when you were born. If it was, subtract the appropriate number of hours from your birth time to con-vert it to GMT. This may give you a different time and/or date of birth.
4 Look up your year of birth in the Annual Sun Sign Changes list. If you were born within these dates and times, you are a Taurean. If you were born outside them, you are either an Arien if you were born in April, or a Gemini if you were born in May.

Two Examples

Here are a couple of examples so you can see how the process works. Let's say we're looking for the Sun sign of Shani, who was born in the UK on 21 April 1944 at 00:15. Start by checking the list of British Summer Time (BST) dates to see if BST was operating at the time of her birth. It was, but you will see that she was born during a phase when two hours had been added, so you have to subtract two hours from her birth time to convert it to GMT. This gives her a birth time of 22:15 on the previous day – therefore, her GMT birthday is 20 April and her GMT birth time is 22:15. Now turn to the Annual Sun Sign Changes list and look up 1944, her year of birth. In that year, the Sun moved into Taurus on 20 April at 05:18, and Shani's GMT birth was later that day, so she is definitely a Taurean. However, if she had been born on 20 April 1944 at the same time, the Sun would still have been in Aries (her GMT birth would be 19 April at 22:15) so she would be an Arien.

But what would her sign be if she were born on 21 May 1928 at 09:15? First, check the dates in the BST list (note the year change from the above example). In 1928, BST began on 22 April at 02:00, which means that Shani's birth time is in BST and has to be converted back to GMT. All you do is subtract one hour, so Shani's birth time in GMT is 08:15. Write this down, so you don't forget it, then look up the Sun Sign dates for 1928 again. This time, look at the May date. The Sun was in Taurus until 21 May at 07:52. This is 23 minutes before Shani's GMT birth time, which means she is a Gemini.

Dates for British Summer Time

If your birthday falls within these dates and times, you were born during BST and will have to convert your birth time back to GMT. To do this, subtract one hour from your birth time. If you were born during a period that is marked *, you must subtract two hours from your birth time to convert it to GMT. All times are given in BST, using the 24-hour clock.

1920 28 Mar, 02:00–25 Oct, 01:59 inc
1921 3 Apr, 02:00–3 Oct, 01:59 inc
1922 26 Mar, 02:00–8 Oct, 01:59 inc
1923 22 Apr, 02:00–16 Sep, 01:59 inc
1924 13 Apr, 02:00–21 Sep, 01:59 inc
1925 19 Apr, 02:00–4 Oct, 01:59 inc
1926 18 Apr, 02:00–3 Oct, 01:59 inc
1927 10 Apr, 02:00–2 Oct, 01:59 inc
1928 22 Apr, 02:00–7 Oct, 01:59 inc
1929 21 Apr, 02:00–6 Oct, 01:59 inc
1930 13 Apr, 02:00–5 Oct, 01:59 inc
1931 19 Apr, 02:00–4 Oct, 01:59 inc
1932 17 Apr, 02:00–2 Oct, 01:59 inc
1933 9 Apr, 02:00–8 Oct, 01:59 inc
1934 22 Apr, 02:00–7 Oct, 01:59 inc
1935 14 Apr, 02:00–6 Oct, 01:59 inc
1936 19 Apr, 02:00–4 Oct, 01:59 inc
1937 18 Apr, 02:00–3 Oct, 01:59 inc
1938 10 Apr, 02:00–2 Oct, 01:59 inc
1939 16 Apr, 02:00–19 Nov, 01:59 inc
1940 25 Feb, 02:00–31 Dec, 23:59 inc
1941 1 Jan, 00:00–4 May, 01:59 inc
1941 4 May, 02:00–10 Aug, 01:59 inc*
1941 10 Aug, 02:00–31 Dec, 23:59 inc
1942 1 Jan, 00:00–5 Apr, 01:59 inc
1942 5 Apr, 02:00–9 Aug, 01:59 inc*
1942 9 Aug, 02:00–31 Dec, 23:59 inc
1943 1 Jan, 00:00–4 Apr, 01:59 inc
1943 4 Apr, 02:00–15 Aug, 01:59 inc*
1943 15 Aug, 02:00–31 Dec, 23:59 inc
1944 1 Jan, 00:00–2 Apr, 01:59 inc
1944 2 Apr, 02:00–17 Sep, 01:59 inc*
1944 17 Sep, 02:00–31 Dec, 23:59 inc
1945 1 Jan, 02:00–2 Apr, 01:59 inc
1945 2 Apr, 02:00–15 Jul, 01:59 inc*
1945 15 Jul, 02:00–7 Oct, 01:59 inc
1946 14 Apr, 02:00–6 Oct, 01:59 inc
1947 16 Mar, 02:00–13 Apr, 01:59 inc
1947 13 Apr, 02:00–10 Aug, 01:59 inc*
1947 10 Aug, 02:00–2 Nov, 01:59 inc
1948 14 Mar, 02:00–31 Oct, 01:59 inc
1949 3 Apr, 02:00–30 Oct, 01:59 inc

1950 16 Apr, 02:00–22 Oct, 01:59 inc
1951 15 Apr, 02:00–21 Oct, 01:59 inc
1952 20 Apr, 02:00–26 Oct, 01:59 inc
1953 19 Apr, 02:00–4 Oct, 01:59 inc
1954 11 Apr, 02:00–3 Oct, 01:59 inc
1955 17 Apr, 02:00–2 Oct, 01:59 inc
1956 22 Apr, 02:00–7 Oct, 01:59 inc
1957 14 Apr, 02:00–6 Oct, 01:59 inc
1958 20 Apr, 02:00–5 Oct, 01:59 inc
1959 19 Apr, 02:00–4 Oct, 01:59 inc
1960 10 Apr, 02:00–2 Oct, 01:59 inc
1961 26 Mar, 02:00–29 Oct, 01:59 inc
1962 25 Mar, 02:00–28 Oct, 01:59 inc
1963 31 Mar, 02:00–27 Oct, 01:59 inc
1964 22 Mar, 02:00–25 Oct, 01:59 inc
1965 21 Mar, 02:00–24 Oct, 01:59 inc
1966 20 Mar, 02:00–23 Oct, 01:59 inc
1967 19 Mar, 02:00–29 Oct, 01:59 inc
1968 18 Feb, 02:00–31 Dec, 23:59 inc
1969 1 Jan, 00:00–31 Dec, 23:59 inc
1970 1 Jan, 00:00–31 Dec, 23:59 inc
1971 1 Jan, 00:00–31 Oct, 01:59 inc
1972 19 Mar, 02:00–29 Oct, 01:59 inc
1973 18 Mar, 02:00–28 Oct, 01:59 inc
1974 17 Mar, 02:00–27 Oct, 01:59 inc
1975 16 Mar, 02:00–26 Oct, 01:59 inc
1976 21 Mar, 02:00–24 Oct, 01:59 inc
1977 20 Mar, 02:00–23 Oct, 01:59 inc
1978 19 Mar, 02:00–29 Oct, 01:59 inc
1979 18 Mar, 02:00–28 Oct, 01:59 inc
1980 16 Mar, 02:00–26 Oct, 01:59 inc
1981 29 Mar, 01:00–25 Oct, 00:59 inc
1982 28 Mar, 01:00–24 Oct, 00:59 inc
1983 27 Mar, 01:00–23 Oct, 00:59 inc
1984 25 Mar, 01:00–28 Oct, 00:59 inc
1985 31 Mar, 01:00–27 Oct, 00:59 inc
1986 30 Mar, 01:00–26 Oct, 00:59 inc
1987 29 Mar, 01:00–25 Oct, 00:59 inc
1988 27 Mar, 01:00–23 Oct, 00:59 inc
1989 26 Mar, 01:00–29 Oct, 00:59 inc
1990 25 Mar, 01:00–28 Oct, 00:59 inc
1991 31 Mar, 01:00–27 Oct, 00:59 inc

1992 29 Mar, 01:00–25 Oct, 00:59 inc
1993 28 Mar, 01:00–24 Oct, 00:59 inc
1994 27 Mar, 01:00–23 Oct, 00:59 inc
1995 26 Mar, 01:00–22 Oct, 00:59 inc
1996 31 Mar, 01:00–27 Oct, 00:59 inc
1997 30 Mar, 01:00–26 Oct, 00:59 inc
1998 29 Mar, 01:00–25 Oct, 00:59 inc

1999 28 Mar, 01:00–31 Oct, 00:59 inc
2000 26 Mar, 01:00–29 Oct, 00:59 inc
2001 25 Mar, 01:00–28 Oct, 00:59 inc
2002 31 Mar, 01:00–27 Oct, 00:59 inc
2003 30 Mar, 01:00–26 Oct, 00:59 inc
2004 28 Mar, 01:00–31 Oct, 00:59 inc

* Subtract two hours from the birth time to convert it to GMT.

Annual Sun Sign Changes

If your birthday falls within these dates and times, you are a Taurean. If you were born in April before the first date and time, you are an Arien. If you were born in May after the second date and time, you are a Gemini. All times are given in GMT, using the 24-hour clock.

1920 20 Apr, 09:40–21 May, 09:21 inc
1921 20 Apr, 15:33–21 May, 15:16 inc
1922 20 Apr, 21:29–21 May, 21:10 inc
1923 21 Apr, 03:06–22 May, 02:46 inc
1924 20 Apr, 08:59–21 May, 08:40 inc
1925 20 Apr, 14:52–21 May, 14:32 inc
1926 20 Apr, 20:37–21 May, 20:14 inc
1927 21 Apr, 02:32–22 May, 02:07 inc
1928 20 Apr, 08:17–21 May, 07:52 inc
1929 20 Apr, 14:11–21 May, 13:47 inc
1930 20 Apr, 20:06–21 May, 19:41 inc
1931 21 Apr, 01:40–22 May, 01:16 inc
1932 20 Apr, 07:28–21 May, 07:06 inc
1933 20 Apr, 13:19–21 May, 12:56 inc
1934 20 Apr, 19:01–21 May, 18:35 inc
1935 21 Apr, 00:51–22 May, 00:24 inc
1936 20 Apr, 06:32–21 May, 06:07 inc
1937 20 Apr, 12:20–21 May, 11:57 inc
1938 20 Apr, 18:15–21 May, 17:50 inc
1939 20 Apr, 23:56–21 May, 23:26 inc
1940 20 Apr, 05:51–21 May, 05:22 inc
1941 20 Apr, 11:51–21 May, 11:22 inc
1942 20 Apr, 17:40–21 May, 17:08 inc
1943 20 Apr, 23:32–21 May, 23:02 inc
1944 20 Apr, 05:18–21 May, 04:50 inc
1945 20 Apr, 11:07–21 May, 10:40 inc

1946 20 Apr, 17:03–21 May, 16:33 inc
1947 20 Apr, 22:40–21 May, 22:09 inc
1948 20 Apr, 04:25–21 May, 03:57 inc
1949 20 Apr, 10:18–21 May, 09:50 inc
1950 20 Apr, 16:00–21 May, 15:28 inc
1951 20 Apr, 21:49–21 May, 21:15 inc
1952 20 Apr, 03:37–21 May, 03:03 inc
1953 20 Apr, 09:26–21 May, 08:52 inc
1954 20 Apr, 15:20–21 May, 14:47 inc
1955 20 Apr, 20:58–21 May, 20:24 inc
1956 20 Apr, 02:44–21 May, 02:12 inc
1957 20 Apr, 08:42–21 May, 08:10 inc
1958 20 Apr, 14:28–21 May, 13:51 inc
1959 20 Apr, 20:17–21 May, 19:42 inc
1960 20 Apr, 02:06–21 May, 01:33 inc
1961 20 Apr, 07:56–21 May, 07:22 inc
1962 20 Apr, 13:51–21 May, 13:16 inc
1963 20 Apr, 19:37–21 May, 18:58 inc
1964 20 Apr, 01:28–21 May, 00:49 inc
1965 20 Apr, 07:27–21 May, 06:50 inc
1966 20 Apr, 13:12–21 May, 12:32 inc
1967 20 Apr, 18:56–21 May, 18:18 inc
1968 20 Apr, 00:42–21 May, 00:06 inc
1969 20 Apr, 06:28–21 May, 05:49 inc
1970 20 Apr, 12:16–21 May, 11:37 inc
1971 20 Apr, 17:55–21 May, 17:15 inc

1972 19 Apr, 23:38–20 May, 23:00 inc
1973 20 Apr, 05:31–21 May, 04:55 inc
1974 20 Apr, 11:20–21 May, 10:36 inc
1975 20 Apr, 17:08–21 May, 16:23 inc
1976 19 Apr, 23:04–20 May, 22:21 inc
1977 20 Apr, 04:58–21 May, 04:14 inc
1978 20 Apr, 10:50–21 May, 10:08 inc
1979 20 Apr, 16:36–21 May, 15:54 inc
1980 19 Apr, 22:23–20 May, 21:42 inc
1981 20 Apr, 04:19–21 May, 03:39 inc
1982 20 Apr, 10:08–21 May, 09:23 inc
1983 20 Apr, 15:51–21 May, 15:06 inc
1984 19 Apr, 21:39–20 May, 20:58 inc
1985 20 Apr, 03:27–21 May, 02:43 inc
1986 20 Apr, 09:13–21 May, 08:28 inc
1987 20 Apr, 14:58–21 May, 14:10 inc
1988 19 Apr, 20:46–20 May, 19:57 inc

1989 20 Apr, 02:40–21 May, 01:53 inc
1990 20 Apr, 08:28–21 May, 07:37 inc
1991 20 Apr, 14:09–21 May, 13:20 inc
1992 19 Apr, 19:58–20 May, 19:12 inc
1993 20 Apr, 01:50–21 May, 01:03 inc
1994 20 Apr, 07:37–21 May, 06:40 inc
1995 20 Apr, 13:22–21 May, 12:34 inc
1996 19 Apr, 19:11–20 May, 18:23 inc
1997 20 Apr, 01:04–21 May, 00:18 inc
1998 20 Apr, 06:58–21 May, 06:05 inc
1999 20 Apr, 12:47–21 May, 11:52 inc
2000 19 Apr, 18:41–20 May, 17:49 inc
2001 20 Apr, 00:37–20 May, 23:44 inc
2002 20 Apr, 06:22–21 May, 05:29 inc
2003 20 Apr, 12:04–21 May, 11:12 inc
2004 19 Apr, 17:51–20 May, 16:59 inc